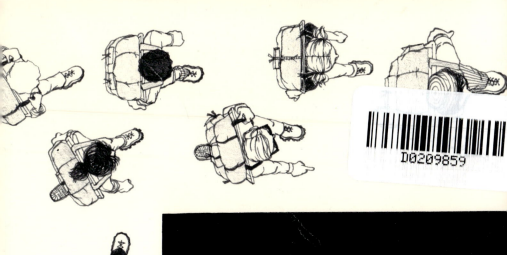

GROUP BACKPACKING
A LEADER'S MANUAL

by
chuck gormley

Illustrations by Mary Phillips

GROUP BACKPACKING
A LEADER'S MANUAL

A Training Guide for both Professional
Program Directors and Volunteers who
Wish to Lead Group Backpacking.

CHUCK GORMLEY

Illustrated by Mary Phillips

GROUPWORK
TODAY, INC.

Post Office Box 258
South Plainfield, N. J. 07080

ISBN - 0916068-08-0

Published by

GROUPWORK
TODAY, INC.
Post Office Box 258
South Plainfield, N. J. 07080

Printed and bound in the U.S.A.

ACKNOWLEDGEMENTS

My thanks go to the many people who helped make this book possible, especially to my wife Aileen for her constructive criticism and constant support. In addition, my thanks go to Mrs. Barbra Sherman and Mrs. Glenda Williams for their typing, proofreading and editorial support and to Professor Ozzie Goering (Lorado Taft Field Campus) for his personal and professional encouragement.

For permission to reprint the following material, thanks are due to:

Journal of Outdoor Education for selections from "Legal Aspects of Adventure Education by Betty van der Smissen, copyright 1975 by Northern Illinois University.

Mazamas for selections from Hypothermia: Killer of the Unprepared by Theodore G. Lathrop, M.D., copyright 1973 by the Mazamas.

The Museum of Science, Boston for selections from Frostbite: What It Is, How to Prevent It, Emergency Treatment by Bradford Washburn, copyright 1963 by the Museum of Science, Boston.

Survival Education Association for selections from Outdoor Living: Problems, Solutions, Guidelines by Eugene Fear, copyright 1971 by Survival Education Association.

Survival Education Association for selections from Surviving the Unexpected Wilderness Emergency by Eugene Fear.

The Mountaineers for selections from Mountaineering First Aid by Dick Mitchell, copyright 1972 by the Mountaineers.

The Mountaineers for selections from Medicine for Mountaineering by James Wilkerson, M.D., copyright 1975 by the Mountaineers.

INTRODUCTION

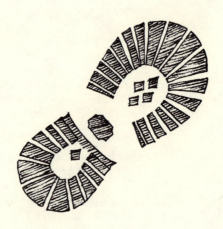

This book is addressed to those who expect to assume the role of a leader on a group backpacking trip.

Group backpacking has gained acceptance as a worthwhile activity from groupwork organizations such as Girl Scouts, Boy Scouts, YW and YMCA's all the way to rehabilitation groups for drug abusers. The Backpacking Boom is on, and with it comes the ever increasing deterioration of the wilderness by the very people who set out to enjoy its pristine beauty.

Solitary backpackers and those who travel with a few choice companions usually resent large backpacking groups. They claim large groups upset their search for solitude and create major environmental damage by their very numbers. They believe this damage to the environment is a result of the local ecology being unable to sustain the overuse created by large groups. To a large extent their claims are true. At least the results cannot be denied. Many trails and campsites in wilderness areas are environmentally imbalanced as a result of human impact upon them. It is the author's belief that the problem is not overuse, as claimed, but rather a case of misuse. Large groups can use the wilderness without greatly upsetting the environment.

Petzolt (1975), former director of the National Outdoor Leadership School, claims, "We can take a group as large as twenty people into the western mountains for five weeks, and I think many other places in the world, without harming the beauty or aesthetics involved." (pp. 4-5).

Most articles appearing in popular magazines for wilderness users support the overuse theory. Yet upon close review their claim of overuse is actually overuse of misuses. This means damage is caused by the repeated use of activities and techniques that are environmentally damaging. Through the use of education and proper leadership, Petzolt can minimize his group's impact on the environment to a point that it would be difficult to locate a former campsite of the group one day after they had camped there. But who should take the responsibility to educate the millions of backpackers who have neither the time nor money to attend such schools? And, how is this education to be conducted? In part, this book is designed to provide backpackers with a guideline for initiating activities and techniques that have minimal environmental impact upon the local ecology. It is the leader's role to help those less knowledgable gain and use this information.

Along with the responsibility for the safety, comfort and enjoyment of the group, it is the leader's ethical responsibility to educate group members in the proper skills and techniques used to conserve the beauty and ecology of the wilderness. Unfortunately, many group leaders have little knowledge or concern for conservation practices. Some still practice skills gained decades ago when there was little concern for protecting and conserving the wilderness. The guidelines presented within this book should help leaders better present up-to-date environmental conservation practices to group members.

While environmental conservation should be a major concern for backpacking groups, safety is the most important concern for group leaders. It is the one aspect of a group backpacking trip for which the leader may be held legally responsible. It cannot be over-emphasized that a leader should insure the safety of all group members during the entire trip. If a leader feels he or she cannot do this, he or she should not assume the responsibility of leadership.

Even the most mundane of activities in which people engage have some degree of risk involved. To avoid accidents one needs a certain amount of physical ability, mental knowledge, proper equipment, and the judgment to use the previous three wisely and safely. It is the leader's responsibility to insure that no member of the group exceeds these limitations. At times it may be necessary for the leader to exercise his or her authority to insure that group members do not exceed their limitations. If this need arises, the leader should not hesitate to wield that authority. Thus a leader should not only be a protector of the wilderness but also a protector of its users.

What then does a person need to know or be, to be considered a proficient leader? This question has been the subject of debate by outdoorsmen for years and will probably continue for years. However, for the sake of completeness, the author has compiled a personal generalized list of skills and personality traits expected of a group backpacking leader.

A potential group leader should be proficient in the following:

1. Planning expeditiously, but thoroughly, a group backpacking trip that is within cost, ability, and time limitations of the group.

2. Demonstrating and explaining to the group the skills and techniques needed to undertake a backpacking trip.

3. Recognizing the skill levels of each group member and helping each member gain those skills and techniques mentioned above at a rate that is comfortable for that person.

4. Communicating with each group member and the group as a whole in a manner which warrants their respect and camaraderie.

5. Relating to the group their impact upon the local environment.

6. Demonstrating and explaining proper environmental precautions and practices that should be exercised before, during, and after all group activities.

7. Adminstering first aid properly.

8. Having the group react properly to an accident or other emergency situation.

9. Recognizing and safely avoiding or negotiating potential physical and climatic hazards.

10. Recognizing and properly responding to any physical or emotional distress experienced by group members.

11. Demonstrating and explaining necessary safety precautions when using and maintaining any and all equipment used on the trip.

12. Relating to the group members the dangers resulting from the misuse or abuse of any and all equipment used on the trip.

13. Demonstrating and explaining safety precautions and procedures associated with any and all skills, techniques, and activities expected

6

of group members.

14.   Relating to the group members the potential dangers resulting from the misuse or lack of use of such proper safety precautions and procedures.

15.   Maintaining and having within the group's possession an adequate "group size" first aid kit.

16.   Familiarity with the contents and use of the first aid kit mentioned above.

17.   Gaining a reasonable knowledge of the physical and emotional limitations of each group member.

18.   Accepting and positively reacting to constructive criticism, no matter what the source!

To help in attaining the skills mentioned in the preceding list, this book is divided into learning objectives. It is the intent of each learning objective to have a leader review the content of the chapter, evaluate its usefulness, and adapt information found useful to his or her own future trip plans.

Chuck Gormley
University of California, San Diego
1978

TABLE OF CONTENTS

EXAMPLES OF FORMS AND HANDOUTS

Appendix

Appendix

CHAPTER 1

PURPOSES FOR A GROUP BACKPACKING TRIP

Objective: To familiarize the leader with different purposes served by a group backpacking trip.

Desired Understanding:

    1. The need to have purposes for a group backpacking trip.

    2. Purposes that may be served by a group backpacking trip.

1.1   1. <u>The Need for Purposes.</u> It is important to have clearly defined purposes for a group backpacking trip. For some people the activity of carrying a heavy pack around the countryside for a week or so is just not enough justification to go backpacking. In determining purposes consider the wants and needs of all the group members and do not necessarily confine the trip to a single purpose.

1.2   2. <u>Common Purposes Served by a Group Backpacking Trip.</u>

1.2A   A. <u>Recreational Backpacking.</u> Backpacking may be an end in itself. Acquiring and using the skills, techniques, and judgment necessary to be self-propelled and independent of civilization are often the major purposes of a backpacking trip.

1.2B   B. <u>Other Recreational Activities.</u> A backpacking trip can serve as a means by which otherwise inaccessible locations may be reached to engage in various recreational activities such as:

    1. Fishing
    2. Rock Climbing
    3. Ice Climbing
    4. Spelunking
    5. Snowshoeing
    6. Cross-country Skiing
    7. Orienteering

1.2C   C. <u>Educational.</u> A backpacking trip may be used as an experiential activity to supplement and/or synthesize formal learning objectives.

1.2D   D. <u>Physical Development.</u> Increasing participant's physical fitness, prior to and during a backpacking trip, may be reason to initiate a group trip.

1.2E   E. <u>Social Development.</u> A backpacking group becomes a "mini-society" in the wilderness. The interdependence of group members necessary for a successful trip may serve as a learning experience for developing social skills.

1.2F   F. <u>Therapeutic.</u> Many counseling and rehabilitation programs are discovering the wilderness as a setting that is conducive to physical and psychological therapy.

1.2G   G. <u>Appreciation Development.</u> Being self-propelled in the wilderness usually provides the time and the environment to better gain and develop an appreciation for the historical, geological, aesthetic, and ecological attributes of the region.

CHAPTER 2

SELECTING GROUP MEMBERS

Objective: To familiarize the leader with different considerations in choosing group members who may have an
effect on the group during a backpacking trip.

Desired Understanding:

1. Possible criteria to consider in choosing group members.

2. Evaluation techniques used to determine a potential
group member's ability to meet the necessary criteria.

3. How potential group members may meet the necessary
criteria.

2.1   1. Possible Criteria Used in Selecting Group Members.

2.1A   A. Does this person have the skills necessary to undertake
trip?

2.1B   B. Does this person have the previous experience necessary
to undertake this trip?

2.1C   C. Does this person have the physical ability to meet the
physical demands imposed by this trip?

2.1D   D. Will this person be an asset to the group?

2.1E   E. Will this person's personality be compatible with the
rest of the group members?

2.1F   F. Does this person have a positive attitude about the group?

2.1G   G. Does this person have a positive attitude about this trip?

2.1H   H. Does this person have a positive attitude about conserving the environment?

2.2   2. Evaluation Techniques. To ascertain the answers to the above
questions, it may be advantageous to have potential group members participate in one or more of the following activities.

2.2A   A. <u>An overnight backpacking trip</u> may be planned in which each person must demonstrate proficiency in the following areas:

     1. Equipment selection, use, and maintenance.

     2. Food planning, packing, and preparation.

     3. The use of map and compass.

     4. Campsite selection, including site locations for tents, latrines, and cooking areas.

     5. Ability to dress and sleep comfortably.

     6. Ability to properly react to a "simulated" emergency situation.

     7. Proper conservation techniques.

     8. Personal and group safety.

2.2B   B. <u>A day trip</u> may be taken in which each person must demonstrate proficiency in the same areas as outlined in section 2.2A. Because the group will not actually be camping overnight, much of the time otherwise spent hiking will be used to demonstrate camp skills and techniques.

2.2C   C. If there is not an opportunity for an overnight trip or day trip, interviews may be arranged between the leader and potential group members. Through an interview a leader may elicit the needed information necessary to answer questions outlined in section 2.1.

2.3   3. <u>Upgrading</u>. Potential group members found lacking in physical ability or skill levels may be helped to meet the necessary criteria by engaging in one or more of the following, leader recommended activities:

2.3A   A. <u>A physical conditioning program.</u>

2.3B   B. <u>Seminars and/or learning experiences</u> pertinent to the areas in which they need help.

2.3C   C. <u>Reading books and magazine articles,</u> selected by the leader, pertinent to the areas in which they need help.

CHAPTER 3

SELECTING TRIP DATES

Objective: To familiarize the leader with different variables that may affect the selection of dates for the trip.

Desired Understanding:

1. How weather conditions may affect the date selection.

2. How the purpose of the trip may affect the date selection.

3. Date selection in relation to previous time commitments.

4. Date selection in relation to pre-trip planning.

3.1   1. <u>Weather conditions</u> may affect the selection of trip dates for the following reasons:

3.1A   A. Extreme weather conditions can negatively affect some group member's abilities and attitudes. The result may be that a trip becomes less safe or less enjoyable than if it were taken under more favorable weather conditions.

3.1B   B. If the weather conditions are unpredictable, it may be of benefit to select an alternate trip date so that if unfavorable weather conditions prevail on the initial trip date, the group can postpone the trip without the necessity of total replanning.

3.2   2. The "<u>purpose</u>" of the trip may dictate the trip dates. If, for example, the group wanted to view the migration of certain species of birds, it may necessitate the group be at a certain location within certain time limits so that the migration may be seen.

3.3   3. <u>Pre-trip planning.</u> There are usually many things that need to be done prior to the trip. In choosing trip dates the leader should allow enough lead time to accomplish these activities. Possible activities are listed below:

3.3A   A. Evaluation of group members

      See section 2.2

21

3.3B   B.   Completion of "Upgrading activities."

See Section 2.3.

3.3C   C.   Acquisition of information concerning potential trip locations.

See section 4.2.

3.3D   D.   Evaluation of information concerning potential trip locations.

See section 4.1.

3.3E   E.   Making all necessary transportation arrangements.

See Chapter 5.

3.3F   F.   Acquisition of all necessary maps and guidebooks.

See section 4.2.

3.3G	G.	Making all campsite reservations.
		See section 4.2E.
3.3H	H.	Acquisition of all fire permits.
		See section 4.2E.
3.3I	I.	Acquisition of all necessary hiking permits.
		See section 4.2E.
3.3J	J.	Acquisition of permission to use private property.
		See section 4.2F.
3.3K	K.	Acquisition of all funds from sponsoring organization.
		See Chapter 12.
3.3L	L.	Acquisition of all funds from group members.
		See Chapter 12.
3.3M	M.	Creation, printing and distribution of all handouts to be used in conjunction with group meetings.
		See section 8.2E.

CHAPTER 4

SELECTING A TRIP LOCATION

Objective: To familiarize the leader with consideration involved in selecting a trip location and selecting a
trail or trails to hike within that location.

Desired Understanding:

1. Major considerations in choosing a location.

2. Major information resources which may aid in "location" and "trail" selection.

3. Types of trail routing systems that may be chosen.

4. Determining "hiking times" to better plan a trip.

5. Necessary data in constructing a "Daily Trip Itinerary."

4.1   1. <u>Major Considerations in Selecting a Trip Location.</u>

4.1A   A.   Does the location offer the geological and ecological
attributes necessary to successfully satisfy the purpose of the
trip?

4.1B   B.   Is the location within reasonable driving distance?

4.1C   C.   Do all group members have the skills and abilities to
undertake a trip at this particular location?

4.1D   D.   Are the expected weather conditions at the location
suitable for the purpose of the trip and the limitations of the
group?

4.2   2. <u>Information Sources.</u>   When selecting a trip location, it is
advantageous and often necessary to obtain and evaluate all
available information concerning potential trip locations.   This
information may help in selecting a location and planning a trip.
The following is a list of information sources that may be of
benefit in choosing a trip location and determining what trail or
trails to hike within that location.

4.2A   A.   <u>U.S. Geological Survey.</u>   This governmental agency can provide the following:

1. <u>Index Map for the States.</u> This booklet will aid in the selection of the proper maps needed for your trip location.

2. "U.S. Geological Survey Topographical Series." While these maps are very accurate in detailing physical features, they are often inaccurate in detailing trail locations and trail shelters. It is best to use these maps in conjunction with local trail maps and guidebooks.

3. Mailing address: U.S. Geological Survey
Distribution Section
Washington, D.C. 20242
(for eastern states)

U.S. Geological Survey
Distribution Section
Federal Center
Denver, Colorado 80225
(for western states)

4.2B B. <u>National Park Service</u>. This governmental agency can provide the following:

1. Maps of all the National Parks.

2. Generalized guidebooks for National Park Users.

3. Generalized rules and regulations for National Park Users.

4. Addresses and telephone numbers of all National Parks.

5. Mailing address: National Park Service
Department of Interior
Washington, D.C. 20240

4.2C C. <u>U.S. Forest Service</u>. This governmental agency can provide the following.

1. Maps of all areas controlled by the U.S. Forest Service.

2. Generalized rules and regulations for users of U.S. Forest Service controlled areas.

3. Addresses and telephone numbers of all areas controlled by the U.S. Forest Service.

4. Mailing address: U. S. Forest Service
                     Department of Agriculture
                     Washington, D. C. 20250

4.2D   D. <u>The National Climatic Center</u>. This governmental agency can provide the following:

1. <u>Climatic Survey of the United States.</u> This is a series of inexpensive booklets featuring the weather histories of local areas within each of the states. Obtaining a booklet covering the location of your trip can aid in estimating the range of weather conditions the group is likely to face for a particular time of the year.

2. Mailing address: The National Climatic Center
                     Federal Building
                     Asheville, North Carolina 28801

4.2E   E. <u>Local Headquarters for National, State, County and Local Parks, Forests, and Recreational Areas.</u> Direct contact with the administrative agency of a location is usually the best source of up-to-date information. Much of the information available may be in the form of free printed material. Other, specific information may be obtained through written requests or telephone conversations. What follows is a list of information that can usually be obtained through these agencies:

1. Maps (USGS and local trail maps).

2. Guidebooks.

3. Rules and regulations for a particular area.

4. Local weather conditions.

5. Trail conditions.

6. Availability of campsites for a particular time of the year and for specific days of the week.

7. Precautions concerning insects, wildlife, and poisonous plants.

8. Water sources along the trail.

9. Equipment requirements and/or recommendations.

10. Potential physical hazards along the trail that should be avoided or negotiated in a precautionary manner.

11. Hiking permit information.

12. Campsite reservation information.

13. Parking information.

14. Fire permit information.

4.2F   F. Private Property Owners. It may be necessary to obtain permission to use private property. If the owner of the property is unknown, his or her identity can usually be obtained at the nearest county clerk's office. The property owner or caretaker can usually provide the following:

1. The same information as outlined in section 4.2E.

2. Expected behavior near private buildings.

3. Expected behavior while crossing fences or passing through gates.

4. Expected behavior around crops, livestock, and machinery.

Note: In written correspondence with private property owners, it is common courtesy to include a stamped, self-addressed envelope when requesting a written reply.

4.2G
    G. Local Equipment Stores. Store owners and/or employees can usually provide the following:

        1. Information concerning the purchase, rental and possible discounts for equipment and trail foods.

        2. Maps (USGS and local trail maps).

        3. Guidebooks.

        4. Resource people who may lend advice in both planning the trip and about the area to be hiked.

4.2H
    H. Local Hiking Clubs (private, public, high school, and college). These organizations may be able to provide the following:

        1. Resource people. See section 4.2G4.

        2. Information concerning the free use or rental of the club's equipment.

        3. Use of the club's maps and guidebooks.

4.2I
    I. Mail Order Equipment Catalogs. These suppliers (see Appendix U) can usually provide information concerning the purchase, rental, and possible discount of equipment, trail foods, maps, and guidebooks.

4.2J
    J. Antelope Camping Equipment. This organization can provide A Trail Profile--How? Why? This informative workbook will aid in the creation of a trail profile, which is a graphic device by which information gathered from USGS maps can be transformed into valuable statistics concerning estimated hiking times. See section 4.4.

4.2K
    K. Pre-Trip Visitation. Much first-hand information can be gathered by visiting a potential trip location. This activity, however, is often impractical if the location is a great distance away.

4.3   3. <u>Trail Routing Systems</u>. In choosing a trail or trails to hike, the group may have a choice of routing systems. What follows is a list of the more common systems.

4.3A   A. <u>There and Back Again</u>. The group may elect to begin hiking on a particular trail or trail system and return along the same trail or trail system. While it is true that all trails look different when traveled in the opposite direction, there is a certain amount of adventure and sense of discovery lost by hiking the same trail twice. Many experienced hikers find this option to be the least desirable.

4.3B   B. <u>Shuttle</u>. By shuttling vehicles and people, the group may attain a situation in which half of the vehicles are parked at the end of the trail and the other half are parked at the beginning of the trail. In this way the group may hike from one place to another and never pass the same place twice. At the end of the hike, the vehicles and people are again shuttled so that all may return home in the same vehicles they came by. This option is somewhat time consuming and may present a parking problem for the vehicles parked at the end of the trail.

4.3C   C. If the group is divided into two smaller groups, both groups may start at opposite ends of the trail. Upon meeting somewhere near the half-way point on the trail, the groups would exchange vehicle keys making it possible for both groups to have transportation at the end of their respective hikes. With this option there are two negative considerations -- suitable parking for vehicles at both locations may present a problem, and there would be a need for two leaders and two sets of group equipment.

4.3D   D. <u>Loop</u>. The most desirable situation is one in which the group begins hiking on a particular trail and returns via another trail to the same starting location thus forming a loop. In this, manner there is need for only one parking location and one leader and the group has the advantage of never having to hike the same trail twice.

4.4   4. <u>Hiking Times.</u> Whether by choice or by necessity, the group may have to reach a specified campsite location each night. Through the use of USGS maps, a "trail profile" and an estimation of the group's hiking speed on flat ground (lineal hiking speed), it is possible to determine the time it will take to reach the specified campsite each day (see Table 1).

Note: If there are any specific learning experiences planned, or if the group is comprised mostly of "beginners," the total time spent on the trail may be half again as long as the actual hiking time. (Petzolt, 1974).

4.5   5. Necessary Data in Constructing a "Daily Trip Itinerary." A "Daily Trip Itinerary" is a detailed plan outlining times and distances to be hiked each day (see Appendix A). At this point in the planning of the trip, the following information should be determined:

1. What time of the day, each day, will the group begin hiking?

2. What time of the day, each day, will the group stop to make camp?

3. What distance will be hiked each day?

4. What are the total elevation gains and losses each day (see section 4.2J)?

Table 1

Estimating Hiking Times: An Example

Known Information:

1. One hour should be added to hiking time for each 1,000 feet of vertical change (up or down) up to an elevation of 7,000 feet above sea level.

2. One and one-half hours should be added to hiking time for each 1,000 feet of vertical change (up or down) between 7,000 feet and 11,000 in elevation above sea level.

3. Two hours should be added to hiking time for each 1,000 feet of vertical change (up or down) above 11,000 feet in elevation above sea level.

4. Starting point (A) is at an elevation of 7,200 feet.

5. Finishing point (B) is at an elevation of 9,600 feet.

6. Lineal distance between point A and point B is 5.5 miles.

Table 1 (continued)

7. Group's estimated lineal hiking speed is 2.5 mph.

8. "Base Time" or normal hiking time without any change in elevation is: lineal distance / estimated lineal hiking speed.

9. "Base Time" =

$$\text{"Base Time"} = \frac{5.5 \text{ miles}}{2.5 \frac{\text{miles}}{\text{hour}}} = 2.2 \text{ hours}$$

10. Vertical changes between point A and point B = (UP: 1,000 ft., 1,200 ft., 600 ft., 1,000 ft; DOWN: 900 ft., 500 ft.) = 5,200 ft. total vertical change.

11. "Vertical Correction" = total vertical change

$$\times \frac{1.5 \text{ hours}}{1,000 \text{ ft.}} = 5,200 \text{ ft.} \times \frac{1.5 \text{ hours}}{1,000 \text{ ft.}} = 7.8 \text{ hours.}$$

12. "Total Hiking Time" = "Base Time" + "Vertical Correction" = 2.2 hours + 7.8 hours = 10 hours.

Conclusion:

For the group to hike a distance of 5.5 miles on flat ground, it would take 2.2 hours; but with 5,200 feet of vertical change in that distance, it would take the group 10 hours to hike. This example makes it obvious that the use of a trail profile can be of great benefit in planning a trip.

Information Sources:

1. U.S. Geological Survey Topographical Series maps.

2. A Trail Profile -- How? Why? (Goddard, 1975).

4.5A   A. In conjunction with the information included in the "Daily Trip Itinerary," the following information should be marked or indicated on all maps and guidebooks:

1. Trailhead parking location.

2. Trailhead starting point for the actual hike if other than the same location as the trailhead parking location.

3. All trails to be hiked.

4. All campsite locations.

5. All major water sources along the trails to be hiked.

6. Potential physical hazards along or near the trails to be hiked.

7. Possible emergency and evacuation routes to the nearest medical and/or rescue services. See section 9. 2A.

8. Finishing point.

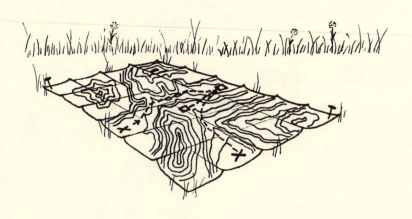

Chapter 5

TRANSPORTATION

Objective: To familiarize the leader with criteria involved in making transportation arrangements for a group backpacking trip.

Desired Understanding:

1. Consideration in planning transportation arrangements.

2. Necessary driver's qualifications.

3. Criteria for selecting a departure location.

4. Criteria for selecting a departure time.

5. Possible unexpected problems along the road.

6. Meal arrangements along the road.

7. Considerations for a return location.

5.1   1. <u>Considerations in Planning Transportation Arrangements</u>.

The following questions need to be considered prior to the trip:

5.1A   A. What is the transportation cost to participants and/or the sponsoring organization?

5.1B   B. What is the minimal number of vehicles required?

5.1C   C. Do the number and types of vehicles chosen for the trip provide adequate comfort for the passengers?

5.1D   D. Do the vehicles chosen have adequate storage space for equipment?

5.1E   E. Is there adequate insurance coverage for all vehicles, drivers, and passengers?

5.1F   F. Will the chosen vehicles require pre-trip servicing and/or maintenance checks?

5.1G   G. Do arrangements need to be made to rent or borrow vehicles?

5.1H   H. Is there adequate safety and maintenance equipment for each vehicle? See Appendix L.

5.2   2. _Driver's Qualifications._ It is the leader's responsibility to assure the group that all drivers have a valid driver's license and adequate liability insurance coverage. See Appendix L.

5.3   3. _Criteria for Selecting a Departure Location._ It may be advantageous to have a single location where all members can meet and depart at the same time. In this way it is possible for all vehicles to travel in a caravan making it easier for the leader to oversee the entire group when traveling to the activity location. In choosing a location, consider the following questions:

5.3A   A. Will the group members be able to find the location easily?

5.3B   B. If the departure time is early in the morning or late in the evening, will the noise made by the group be a nuisance to other people?

5.3C   C. Does the location have shelter and warmth for the group members?

5.3D   D. Does the location have rest rooms available for the group members' use?

5.3E   E. Is there a telephone at the location available for the group members' use?

5.3F   F. Does the location offer adequate, safe parking for all vehicles?

5.4   4. _Criteria for Selecting a Departure Time._ In choosing a departure time, consider the following questions:

5.4A   A. Are all group members available to leave at the proposed time?

5.4B   B. Will the proposed departure time present the group with any likely traffic problems along the route of travel?

5.4C   C.   Upon arriving at the trailhead parking location, will the group start hiking or will they camp at a "car campsite," near the parking location, for the night?

5.4D   D.   Will time be needed to conduct business with the administrative agency or with the land owner at the location upon arrival?

5.4E   E.   Will time be needed to shuttle people and vehicles to various parking locations? (See section 4.3B).

5.5   5.   <u>Possible Unexpected Problems Along the Road.</u> Though no one plans to have problems along the road, at times they do arise. To avoid possible confusion and/or ill feelings among group members, a policy should be developed to deal with the following problems <u>before</u> they occur:

5.5A   A.   Who will pay for towing charges in the event of a vehicle breakdown?

5.5B   B.   Who will pay for "road service" charges in the event of a vehicle breakdown?

5.5C   C.   Who will pay for repair charges in the event of a vehicle breakdown?

5.5D   D.   Who will pay the fine for a "moving" traffic violation?

5.5E   E.   Who will pay the fine for a "nonmoving" traffic violation?

5.5F   F.   In the event of a vehicle being unable to continue due to a breakdown, who will pay for the group members to use public transportation or to rent a vehicle to continue the trip or to return home?

5.6   6.   <u>Meal Arrangements Along the Road.</u> Should the trip to and from the activity location be lengthy, it may be necessary to make meal arrangements for the group. Several options are listed below:

5.6A   A.   Each individual bring his or her own food.

5.6B   B.   Small groups of people bring food for themselves.

5.6C   C. Food is planned for and provided for the whole group.

5.6D   D. Meals are purchased along the way for the entire group.

5.6E   E. Individuals will purchase their meals at roadside restaurants.

5.7   7. <u>Considerations for a Return Location.</u>   If it is decided that the group will return to a single location, the criteria used to choose a departure location (section 5.3) should be used to choose a return location. It is, however, a common practice to drop the group members off at their homes or at a location of their choice.

Chapter 6

FOOD AND COOKING

Objective: To introduce the leader to the considerations involved in planning, purchasing, packaging, packing,
and preparing foods for group backpacking trips.

Desired Understanding:

1. Different types of "cook group" arrangements.

2. Types of food especially suited for backpacking trips.

3. Major considerations in choosing foods for a backpacking trip.

4. The advantage of using a "Menu Planner."

5. The process of food repackaging, packaging, and
packing food.

6. The advantages and disadvantages of using a stove for
cooking meals on a backpacking trip.

7. The use of fires for the preparation of meals on a
backpacking trip.

6.1   1. Types of Cook Groups.

6.1A   A. Individual. With this option each group member is responsible for the planning, purchasing, packing, and preparation of his meals. The only real advantages of this option are
that each group member is assured of having menus of his
choice and is able to prepare the meals the way he personally
wants them prepared. The disadvantages include the amount
of time spent having each person plan, purchase, pack, and
prepare the food and having each member responsible for
carrying a complete cook kit and possibly a stove. There may
also be a need to have more cooking fires than is in keeping
with sound environmental practices in the "back country."

6.1B   B. Small Group. With this option the whole group is divided into small groups and as a unit these small groups will
plan, purchase, pack, and prepare all food for their group.

43

This option is usually the best choice for large groups in that people with similar eating habits may form groups in which they can have the menus of their choice and not have to do all the work, individually, in planning, purchasing, packing, and preparing the food. These small groups usually number from two to six people.

6.1C C. <u>Whole Group.</u> With this option the planning, purchasing, packing, and preparation of all food are shared by the entire group. Committees are usually formed to take the responsibility for the above mentioned duties. The advantage of this option is that food may be purchased in bulk, thus reducing costs and the time involvement of each person is much less than in the other two options. The disadvantage is that members may have to eat meals that are both planned and prepared by other members, possibly with different eating habits than themselves.

6.2 2. <u>Types of Foods Especially Suited for Backpackers.</u> Backpackers must carry all their equipment and food on their backs; thus in choosing foods they usually require items that are light in weight, easy to prepare, and exhibit little or no spoilage. There are three types of food processing methods whose products meet those specifications: sun-drying, artificial dehydration, and "freeze-drying." Most of the resultant products can be purchased at outdoor equipment stores or through mail order equipment suppliers. What follows are brief descriptions of the three methods of processing.

6.2A A. <u>Sun-drying.</u> This is a natural process in which food is simply put out in the light and heat of the sun to dry. The resultant product weighs about 70% to 80% of its original weight, and is shriveled drastically. It is almost impossible to reconstitute it to its original size, shape, or texture. Most sun-dried foods are either fruit or meat. Examples include such items as raisins and beef jerky.

6.2B B. <u>Artificial Dehydration.</u> In this process food is dehydrated with the use of machines which control both the temperature and the humidity at which the food is processed. The product has about 5% to 20% of its original moisture content, making it very light in weight in comparison to the original unprocessed food. Reconstitution of the food takes from one-half to four hours, depending on the constitution of the particular food. Most dehydrated food needs to be added to boiling water as part of the preparation process. There are, however, new dehydrated foods that are packaged in special plastic bags. Water is added to the contents and the bag is then resealed. The bag is then immersed in boiling water until the food is fully cooked, thus eliminating the need to clean pots and pans.

6.2C   C. "Freeze-drying." This is another mechanical drying process. Food is placed in an airtight container and frozen to an extremely low temperature. At around -50° F. the food is introduced to radiant heat and a vacuum. This process causes all frozen moisture in the food to be sublimated away. The product retains the same size and shape of the original product but has only about 3% of the moisture content. Reconstitution is accomplished by adding hot water to the food. The preparation time is short and there is little or no clean-up needed. The only drawback to freeze-dried foods is the cost, which is at least twice that of similar dehydrated foods.

6.2D   D. Foods Purchased from Supermarkets. This is not a method of processing foods; however, its inclusion seems appropriate to mention here. Supermarkets are a logical choice for backpackers on a tight budget. With a bit of careful planning, the grocer's shelves can provide nutritious, lightweight, easy-to-prepare meals at a much lower cost than those items mentioned above.

6.3   3. Major Considerations in Choosing Foods for a Backpacking Trip.

6.3A   A. Palatability. This simply means, "how the food tastes." All other considerations will have little meaning if the person will not eat the food because he or she does not like the taste of it. It would be reasonable to assume that if a person will eat a certain food at home and enjoy it, he or she will probably enjoy the same food on a backpacking trip. A backpacking trip is no place to experiment with food! If you are not sure of the palatability of a certain food, try it at home first.

6.3B   B. Availability of Water. There may be situations on the trail or in camp where water is scarce. If this situation is known ahead of time (see section 4.2E), the group may elect to carry extra water or to plan a menu that requires little or no water for the meal preparation.

45

6.3C C. Ease of Preparation. If a meal requires many steps in preparation or if the preparation time is long, cooking may become an ordeal rather than an enjoyable activity. This is especially true if the group has just had a long hard hike or if it is raining, snowing, windy, or cold.

6.3D D. Spoilage. Most "sun-dried," "dehydrated," or "freeze-dried" foods will not spoil if they are kept in waterproof containers. Fresh foods, on the other hand, need special care (refrigeration) and even then they only have a limited life before spoilage begins.

6.3E E. Bulk or Volume. At times, space for packing food becomes limited, especially on long trips. As a rule, dehydrated foods take up the least amount of volume, sun-dried foods rate second, while fresh foods and freeze-dried foods are the most voluminous.

Volume need not be a major problem if food is packed in the following manner: Pack all food in a waterproof nylon bag and strap it to the top of the packframe. In this way the food will not need any packing space in the pack. It also allows the weight of the food to be carried above the body's center of gravity, thus conserving more energy than if it were packed lower on the frame and farther away from the line of the center of gravity.

6.3F F. Nutrition. Except for very lengthy trips, nutrition should be of little worry as long as each person receives an adequate amount of calories per day. These calories should be in the form of carbohydrates for quick energy, protein for slower activated calories, and fats for very slow activating calories.

Few experts agree on the exact amount of calories a backpacker should consume per day. Much depends on the metabolism of each individual and the amount of energy needed for each day's activities. A rough estimate would be: 3,700 calories per person per day for summer backpacking; and 4,500 calories per person per day for winter backpacking (Pallister, 1974). Many packaged foods have the calorie content on the packaging label. The calorie content of many fresh foods can be found in reference books designed for dieters (see appendix V).

6.3G   G. <u>Weight</u>. With adequate pre-planning, a backpacker can receive the amount of calories mentioned above and keep the weight of food per person per day to $2\frac{1}{2}$ pounds in the summer and 3 pounds in the winter.

6.3H   H.   <u>Cost.</u> It would be reasonable to assume that items purchased at the supermarket will cost less than those same items, processed and packaged differently, sold by outdoor equipment stores or through mail order suppliers. The consumer is paying for the special processing of the foods.

6.3I   I.   <u>Cold Meals.</u> At times it may be convenient or necessary to have meals that require no cooking and little or no preparation time. Such would be the case for most trail lunches. The leader should make the group aware of those types of planned meals prior to the menu planning activities so that the group can plan their meals accordingly.

6.4   4. <u>The Advantage of Using a "Menu Planner."</u> A "Menu Planner" is a record keeping form used for each meal. In planning the meals, all pertinent information concerning nutritional values, weights, and costs is recorded to insure, upon review, that the group members are receiving nutritional meals that are within the chosen weight and cost limits (see Appendix G).

6.5   5. <u>The Process of Food Packing and Repackaging.</u> After all
the menus have been planned and all the food is purchased, it
may be necessary to repackage some foods, and to package all
foods into meals. This will eliminate some bulk and weight by
eliminating unnecessary packaging material and also keep all
food in some type of organization. What follows are step-by-
step instructions on how to repackage and pack food for a backpacking trip:

6.5A   A. Divide all food into two categories:

            1. All staples and condiments (spices, coffee, flour,
                etc.

            2. All other food items.

6.5B   B. Each staple and condiment should be repackaged, individually, into plastic bags with the contents of each bag
labeled.

6.5C   C. All individually bagged staples and condiments should
be bagged together in one large plastic bag and labeled "Staples
and Condiments."

6.5D   D. All remaining food items should be repackaged, individually, into plastic bags (along with preparation instructions)
with the contents of each bag labeled.

6.5E   E. These items should be grouped so as to create individual meals.

6.5F   F. All items for each meal should be placed in a large
plastic bag and labeled: breakfast, lunch, or supper.

6.5G   G. All meal packages should be grouped by the day and
date they are to be eaten.

6.5H   H. All meals for each particular day should be placed in
a large plastic bag and labeled as to the day of the week and
date to be eaten.

6.5I   I. The result is a bag for each day plus a bag for staples
and condiments.

6.5J   J. Throughout the repackaging and packing process, all
unnecessary packaging should be discarded.

6.6   6. The Advantages and Disadvantages of Using a Stove for
Cooking Meals on a Backpacking Trip. Backpacking stoves
come in a variety of styles. They use either white gas, kero-
sene, or bottled fuels such as butane or propane. There are
at least 30 different stoves on the market today designed for
backpackers and other outdoorsmen. It is not within the scope
of this thesis to discuss the merits of the different stoves;
rather, what follows is an overview of the advantages and disadvantages of using any stove for cooking meals on a backpacking trip.

6.6A   A. Advantages.

          1. Stoves are usually dependable in most weather con-
             ditions.

          2. Cooking times, when using stoves, are usually less
             than when using fires.

          3. There is no need to depend on the local environment
             for fuel.

          4. Stoves have much less of a local environment impact
             than do fires.

6.6B   B. Disadvantages.

          1. Stoves are costly.

          2. Stoves and fuel do add weight to the pack.

          3. When using a stove, meals must be cooked in se-
             quence since most backpacking stoves have only one
             burner.

6.6C   C. General Safety Considerations When Using Stoves.

          1. The fueling of stoves should be done well away from
             the campsite.

          2. Only in emergency situations should a stove be used
             inside of a tent and at no time should a stove be
             started in a tent.

6.7   7. The Use of Fires for the Preparation of Meals on a Backpacking Trip. Camp fires have been banned in many areas. This is due in part to the problem of forest fires being caused by unattended or out-of-control campfires. It is also an attempt to stop the environmental destruction caused by the overharvesting of fire wood from the forest's floor. Dead as well as living trees have an important function in the ecosystem. If fires are permitted and if there is sufficient dead wood for a fire without upsetting the local ecology, then a fire may be used for cooking. What follows are descriptions of how fires may be constructed so as to have a minimal impact on the environment.

6.7A   A. On Mineral Soil with no organic material present, dig a shallow pit to contain the fire. After the fire has been extinguished, replace the soil so that it cannot be seen that a fire was once there.

6.7B   B. On Organic Soil, dig a small pit to the depth where mineral soil is reached, to contain the fire. After the fire has been extinguished, replace all soil and sod so that it cannot be seen that a fire was once there.

6.7C   C. On a Rock. If the ground is too moist for a fire or if the organic soil is too deep, a fire can be built on top of a flat rock. The rock should be covered with two to three inches of mineral soil so that it will not be scarred by the fire or crack from the heat. After the fire is extinguished, the remains of the fire should be buried so that it cannot be seen that a fire has been built on the rock.

6.8   8. Fire "Do's."

6.8A   A. Carry out all unburnable material, even those items left by other hikers.

6.8B   B. Try to burn all coals completely.

6.8C   C. Scatter all reserve wood piles so that they are not noticeable.

6.8D   D. Extinguish all fires to a point that the ashes can be stirred with bare hands.

6.8E   E. Cover the fire pit so that it cannot be seen that a fire was once there.

6.9   9. Fire "Do Nots."

6.9A   A. Build a fire near the shore of any water source or place of beauty.

6.9B   B. Build a fire under or around any trees or bushes.

6.9C   C. Use rocks for a fire ring.

6.9D   D. Put unburnable material (including aluminum) in the fire.

6.9E   E. Leave a fire unattended at any time.

6.9F   F. Build fires against trees (living or dead) or rocks.

Chapter 7

EQUIPMENT

Objective: To familiarize the leader with the need for proper
equipment on a backpacking trip.

Desired Understanding:

1. Reasons for having and maintaining the proper equipment.

2. The need to seek advice.

3. The need for equipment lists.

Note: It is not within the scope of this book to discuss
individual pieces of equipment. There exist many fine
books on this subject. Please refer to Appendix V for a
listing of those books.

7.1   1. Reasons for Having the Proper Equipment. A backpacking
trip is supposed to be both safe and enjoyable. By selecting
the proper amount, type, and quality of equipment and by knowing how to properly use and maintain that equipment, a backpacker can help insure both these goals.

7.2   2. The Need to Seek Advice. Even though the leader and some
or all of the group members may be experienced backpackers,
it may be necessary to seek advice in selecting equipment to
use for a particular location for a particular time of the year.
This advice may be obtained from one or more of the following:

7.2A   A. Administrative agency at the location of the trip.

7.2B   B. Persons with previous experience at the same location
and at the same time of year.

7.2C   C. Guidebooks for the area. Often guidebooks have advice concerning equipment to use for the particular area.

7.3   3. Equipment Lists. It is necessary to create and distribute
a "Personal Equipment List" to each of the group members.
For them it will serve as a reminder of the equipment that
they must obtain for the trip, and for the leader it will serve

as a check-list for inspecting each person's equipment prior to the trip. See Appendix H.

The use, maintenance, and packing of all required equipment should be demonstrated to the group members along with advice on where they may obtain the equipment if they do not already have it.

A "Group Equipment List" should be created and distributed to all group members. This will serve as a reminder of the equipment available for all group members' use and for the leader it will serve as a reminder of who is carrying what group equipment. Again, all equipment should be demonstrated to the group members. See Appendix I.

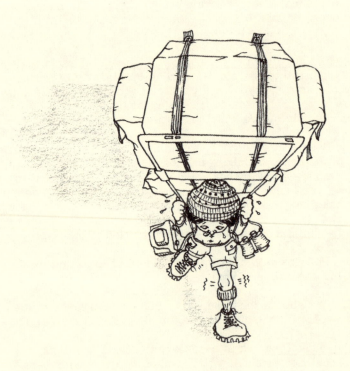

Chapter 8

GROUP MEETINGS

Objective: To acquaint the leader with pertinent agenda for group meetings.

Desired Understanding:

1. A reason for "Meeting # 1."

2. A proposed agenda:

    a. The leader's role.

    b. The assistant leader's role.

    c. The group member's role.

    d. Types of handouts used in conjunction with, or to supplement, group discussions and demonstrations.

3. A reason for "Meeting # 2."

4. A proposed agenda:

    a. Distribution of group equipment and food.

    b. Personal equipment inspection.

    c. Arranging for help.

8. 1   1. A Reason for "Meeting # 1." A group meeting should be held as soon as all the necessary information concerning the trip is gathered and printed. At this meeting there will usually be quite a bit of information to be passed on to group members. Although handouts should be used to expedite and disseminate much of the information, the leader is still the prime source of information. By being well organized, expedient, and willing to entertain questions from the group members, the leader will help present himself or herself as a person with whom the group members can feel confident and secure.

8. 2   2. Proposed Agenda.

8.2A　　　　A. <u>The Leader's Role</u>. It should be emphasized to the group members that since the leader is morally, if not legally, responsible for the safety of the group and the success of the trip, his or her word is final and should be obeyed. Democratic discussions, and even debates, are often welcomed; however, the leader <u>must</u> have the final word on all matters concerning the safety of the group.

8.2B　　　　B. <u>Assistant Leader's Role.</u> An assistant leader should be chosen by the leader prior to the meeting. Group members should be made aware of this person's responsibilities which include aiding the leader when necessary or when requested, and leading the group back to safety should anything happen to the leader.

8.2C　　　　C. <u>Group Member's Role</u>. Group members should be made aware that once they have joined the group they may no longer remain autonomous. They must, at times, sacrifice personal whims and comforts for the good of the group. They must be aware of personal idiosyncracies that may not be appreciated by the group, and try to change them if possible. An awareness of individual differences among group members and an understanding of these differences will aid in becoming a good group member.

　　　　Certain behaviors expected of individual group members and the group as a whole should be discussed at this meeting. Petzolt (1974) devotes an entire chapter to expedition behavior. His explanations of various expected behaviors should be reviewed by the leader and passed on to the group.

8.2D　　　　D. <u>Types of Handouts Used in Conjunction with, or to Supplement Group Discussions and Demonstrations.</u>

Note: Of the handouts listed, the following should be distributed to the group members to fill out and return at some predetermined time.

　　1. "Liability Waiver."

　　2. "Parent Permission Slip and Medical Release Form."

　　3. "Personal Reference Sheet."

　　1. "<u>Liability Waiver.</u>" This is a statement of intent,

58

signed by the participant or his/her legal guardian, releasing the leader and the sponsoring organization from any and all legal responsibility for the participant's physical safety and the safety of his or her personal property. While a "Liability Waiver" is not entirely binding in a court of law, it is a signed statement showing that the participant was fully aware of the leader's and sponsoring organization's position and under those conditions he/she freely chose to go on the trips. This waiver does not, however, negate the possibility of a law suit resulting from negligence on the part of the leader or the sponsoring organization. (See Appendix E.)

Very little printed information is available concerning the actual legal responsibilities of the group leader. What information the author has been able to find is included in Appendix U. The leader should read this information carefully before he or she assumes any leadership responsibilities.

2. "Parent Permission Slip, and Medical Release Form." This form is designed to allow the leader to monetarily aid an "underaged" group member in the event of an emergency and to insure that all "minors" have parental permission to go on the trip. (See Appendix D.)

3. "Personal Reference Sheet." The information will inform the leader, physician, or legal authorities of each group member's next of kin in case of an emergency. Also, it will inform the above mentioned persons of a group member's allergies, medications, and handicaps, if any. (See Appendix F.)

4. "Group Directory." This form is designed to inform all members of the names, addresses, telephone numbers, and cook group of all other members should they have a need to contact them at some time prior to or after the trip. It may also be used as a "passenger list." (See Appendix C.)

5. "Trip Itinerary Sheet." This item should cover all the necessary logistical information needed by the group members. (See Appendix A.)

6. "Daily Itinerary Sheets." This item will give the group members an approximation of each day's plans on the trail. (See Appendix B.)

7. USGS Maps, Trail Maps, Guidebooks. It is necessary for all group members to have a map so that in the event that a member becomes lost he or she may plot locations and have an additional resource when deciding his/her plan of action. The ability to act properly should be evaluated in one of the techniques outlined in section 2.2.
   a. All maps and guidebooks should have all important information highlighted or otherwise indicated. (See section 4.5)

8. "Rules and Regulations." Rules and regulations for a particular area can usually be obtained in quantity from the administrating agency of the area. If on private property, it may be necessary to make copies from the information given by the landowner.

9. Plants and Animals. Precautions concerning poisonous plants and potentially dangerous animals can usually be obtained from the area's administrative agency; however, it may be necessary to have this information reprinted in quantity for distribution to all group members.

10. Hypothermia. If the expected weather conditions for the trip include temperatures below 50° F., it will be necessary to make the group members aware of the dangers of hypothermia. Many free and inexpensive pamphlets are available on this subject. (See Appendix O.)

11. Frostbite. If the group expects to encounter temperatures below freezing, the group should be made aware of the dangers of frostbite. For literature on this subject see Appendix P.

12. Thermal Injuries. Thermal injuries can occur in winter as well as summer. It is difficult to dramatize or demonstrate the effects of thermal injuries; thus the subject should be supplemented with pertinent handout literature. (See Appendix Q.)

13. <u>First Aid Kits.</u> All group members should have an outline of the contents and their uses for both the "group first aid kit" and all "personal first aid kits." (See Appendixes J and K.)

14. <u>"Response to an Accident" Sheets.</u> Mitchell (1972) outlines how to react to an accident regardless of the time, location or extent of the accident and regardless of the size or ability of the group (pp. 15-18). The procedures outlined by Mitchell can and should be practiced by the entire group prior to the trip. (See Appendix M.)

15. <u>"Accident Report Form."</u> In conjunction with the "Response to an Accident" outline, Mitchell also advises the use of accident report forms. He recommends the leader fill out two copies of this form in the event members of the group are sent out to obtain help. One copy accompanies the messengers so the proper authorities will have all available information that may help in sending the group proper help. The second copy should be retained by the leader. (See Appendix N.)

16. <u>"Psychological Problems" Handout.</u> Many psychological problems may arise during an emergency situation along the trail or even on an otherwise uneventful trip. One of the major advantages in combating or negotiating these situations is to have an understanding of them prior to their occurrence. This handout is designed to provide the group members with an understanding. (See Appendix R.)

17. <u>Group Equipment List.</u> See section 7.3. (See Appendix I.)

18. <u>Personal Equipment List.</u> See section 7.3. (See Appendix H.)

19. <u>Menu Planner.</u> See section 6.4. (See Appendix G.)

8.3   3. <u>A Reason for "Meeting # 2."</u> This meeting should be held one or two days prior to the trip. Its purpose is to distribute group equipment and food and to inspect all group members' personal equipment. Also, any last minute details or questions may be dealt with at this meeting.

8.4   4.   A Proposed Agenda.

8.4A   A.   Personal Equipment Inspection. All personal equipment should be inspected by the leader or assistant leader to
insure that all group members have the proper amount, type,
and quality of equipment. It will also be necessary to weigh all
group members' equipment to insure that they are not carrying
too much weight. The maximum weight of personal equipment
to be carried by each person is strictly a judgmental decision
to be made by the leader. If a "rule of thumb" is necessary,
use this rule: A person of "average strength" should be able to
carry about one-third of his/her body weight. (Manning, 1972.)

8.4B   B.   Distribution of Group Equipment and Food. All group
equipment and food should be distributed to group members at
this time so that they may pack everything in their packs prior
to the trip. Some group members may have the physical ability
to carry comfortably heavier loads than others. As long as the
total weight of all members' personal equipment is within the
predetermined weight limits, all group gear and food need not be
distributed equally.

8.4C   C.   Arranging for Help. On or about the time of this meeting the leader should present a "Trip Itinerary," all "Daily Itin-
eraries," and a group directory to a responsible person. The
leader should inform this person that if he or she is not contact-
ed before a certain time on a certain day that he/she should contact the proper authorities to send help to the group. It is the
leader's responsibility to notify this person as soon as possible
after the finish of the hike. The leader should also allow enough
time in setting the time and day that help is to be requested, for
unforeseen delays the group may encounter that might slightly
delay the expected finish time of the hike.

          It may be possible to leave the information with the adminis-
trative agency of the area in which the group will be hiking. This
should be prearranged so that the leader will be assured that
someone will be there to receive the information when the group
arrives at the activity location.

Chapter 9

TRAIL ACTIVITIES AND TECHNIQUES

Objective: To familiarize the leader with activities and techniques that are best experienced along the trail.

Desired Understanding:

1. The leader's role as a teacher on the trail.

2. Common activities and techniques that can be used as learning experiences along the trail.

9.1   1. <u>The Leader's Role as a Trail Teacher.</u>   Seminars and printed handouts are useful in helping group members prepare for a backpacking trip; however, much learning that they will carry with them on future trips is that which takes place on the trip itself. This is to say, learning through direct experience is often the most effective method of learning.

It is the leader's responsibility to help all group members learn the fundamental skills and techniques needed to safely, successfully, and enjoyably undertake a backpacking trip. Much information can be gained on the trail, but the leader must be cautious not to overburden members with information. He should choose opportune times or locations to introduce a skill, technique, or attitude.

9.2   2. <u>Common Activities and Techniques That Can Be Used as Learning Experiences Along the Trail.</u>   The following is an outline and brief description of activities and techniques that may be used to help the group members have a safe, successful, and enjoyable trip.

9.2A   A. <u>Orientation of Maps.</u>   The leader should emphasize to the group the importance of knowing their location at all times. Every group member should orient his or her map with the use of a compass. This exercise should take place at the trailhead before the hike actually begins and be repeated periodically throughout the hike. The following is a list of pertinent reasons for emphasizing this exercise.

1. If each individual knows his or her present location, he/she is <u>never</u> lost. He or she may indeed

be at a location other than where he/she should be, but not lost.

2. In case of an emergency, if escape routes are necessary for going for outside help or for expedient evacuation, knowing your exact location will help in planning the safest and/or fastest route out.

3. Negotiating the planned route of travel is less confusing when your present location is known.

4. It is usually psychologically comforting to know your present location.

9.2B   B. <u>Hoisting a Pack.</u> The leader should demonstrate proper methods of hoisting and lowering a pack to and from a hiker's back and explain the reasons for using these methods. This is another exercise that is best done before the hike actually begins. While most hikers assume they know how to hoist and lower a pack, they may be using unsafe or energy-wasting methods. Petzolt (1974) and Walbridge (1973) have developed safe, efficient methods for hoisting and lowering heavy packs. These methods should be known to the leader so that he or she can pass the information on to the group members.

9.2C   C. <u>Line of March.</u> At the outset of every hike the leader should emphasize to the group the importance of having a line of march. In a line of march, one person is chosen to lead the group, set the pace, and choose the route of travel. He or she is called the "lead person." Another person is chosen to be the last person in line or "end person." His or her responsibilities are to insure that no one falls behind the group and to request a slower pace or a stop should he or she feel a hiker is showing signs of extreme tiredness or fatigue. By rotating these positions, all group members may have the experience of assuming those responsibilities.

9.2D   D. <u>Disposing of Body Wastes.</u> This lesson should take place before the actual need arises, if possible. The leader should explain to the group the proper techniques for disposing of body wastes. The following are descriptions of the more accepted methods:

1. To urinate, the hiker should be at least 30 yards from the nearest trail, campsite, or water source. He or

she should choose a location which is not susceptible to run-off during a rain.

2. To defecate, the hiker should be at least 30 yards from the nearest trail, campsite, or water source. A small hole should be dug about 6 to 10 inches deep but not going below the organic level of the soil. After elimination, the toilet paper used should be burned and the soil returned to the hole. In this manner the feces will quickly be absorbed by the organic soil.

9.2E   E. <u>Blister Check.</u> The leader should emphasize to the group the need to keep their feet in healthy working order. Nothing can ruin a backpacking trip faster than sore feet. The leader should encourage the group members to examine their feet at most stops. This is especially true for "beginner" hikers and those persons wearing new boots.

If a blister has developed, it should be cleansed and drained. Then it should be surrounded by a "doughnut" of moleskin to prevent further pressure and friction on the injured area. If a blister has not developed but an area of the foot is sore or irritated, the same "moleskin doughnut" technique should be employed.

9.2F   F. <u>Rhythmic Breathing and the Rest Step.</u> The leader should demonstrate and explain to the group members the energy-conserving uses of rhythmic breathing and the rest step when employed on uphill hikes. All too often hikers are inclined to go charging up a hill only to end up at the top, panting for air and in need of a rest. These short bursts of energy are very draining.

A hiker practicing rhythmic breathing may seem to be traveling much slower than those persons racing up hills, but in the long run he or she will have the energy reserves to continue hiking when others are finished for the day. The idea is simple though it requires some practice before it is mastered. Rhythmic breathing is the practice of maintaining the same breath rate going uphill as is maintained on level ground. This of course means slowing the pace when going uphill, but at the top the hiker should not be out of breath and not require a rest stop.

In going uphill and practicing rhythmic breathing, a hiker may also want to employ the rest step to further conserve energy. This practice is merely pausing between each forward stride. Again this practice will further slow the pace down when going uphill, but in the long run more reserves of energy will be made available for the hiker to continue on when others are worn out.

The leader may elect to introduce these practices after the group has had the opportunity to hike up a hill at their own chosen pace. In this way the group will usually accept the lesson more readily.

9.2G
G. Switchbacks. The leader should familiarize the group with the effects that cutting across switchbacks have in causing trail erosion. A switchback is a trail that zigzags back and forth as it goes up or down steep inclines to retard the trail erosion caused by rain run-off. Cutting across switchbacks will cause the beginning of a new trail that is more susceptible to erosion.

9.2H
H. Litter and Garbage. The leader should emphasize to the group the need to keep the wilderness free of litter and garbage. Should the group come across litter or garbage along the trail or when passing through a campsite, the leader should explain the need for hikers to carry out not only their own litter and garbage but also the litter and garbage of other less considerate hikers. This topic can lead to further discussion of how people misuse and abuse the wilderness. In working with younger hikers, a reward for the most litter carried out is often an incentive to have the group carry out as much litter and garbage as possible.

Note: The following topics deal with stops the group may make during a hike:

9.2I
I. Number and Frequency of Stops. The leader should notify the group members prior to the trip that the hike will be slow and that stops will be called frequently, or that there will be few stops in order for the group to cover more distance or to spend more time in camp.

There is no set number of stops for any given hike, nor is there a standard time frequency at which stops should be called. Group members will, however, be more comfortable if they have some idea of what to expect ahead of time.

9.2J   J. <u>Rest Stops.</u> The group should be made aware that if a member requests and/or requires a stop because he or she needs to rest, the pace of the group needs to be slowed so that that person can hike at a comfortable speed and not require further rest stops. The group should try to hike at a pace that is comfortable for even the slowest hiker.

9.2K   K. <u>Water Stops.</u> The leader should familiarize the group members with the necessity to avoid becoming dehydrated. (See Appendix Q.) Dehydration is a problem often faced by backpackers. All group members should be encouraged to drink lots of water as often as possible. A quick stop at a stream for a drink of water should not seriously hinder the group's hiking time.

9.2L   L. <u>Activity or Educational Stops.</u> If the leader or the group has planned group activities, educational or other, to engage in while on the trip, stops should be called at an opportune time and/or location for such activities.

9.2M   M. <u>Eating.</u> Group members should be made aware that everyone has different eating habits and that some people enjoy stopping for a snack or for lunch along the trail. This is a justified reason for requesting a stop.

9.2N   N. <u>Picture Taking and Other Important Matters.</u> The leader should encourage group members to stop along the trail to take photographs, sketch, write, or merely relax and enjoy the surroundings. He or she should relate to the group members how these activities may help them gain a better insight into the workings of nature and their personal relation to it.

9.2O   O. <u>Teachable Moments.</u> At any time the leader or any group member encounters some interesting bit of information, a halt should be called to share that information or experience with the rest of the group.

9.2P   P. <u>Safety Stops.</u> The leader should emphasize to the group the need for <u>anyone</u> to call an immediate halt should a safety hazard be recognized or experienced. This type of stop is called in the event of an accident, upon encountering a potential physical hazard along the trail, for frostbite checks, etc.

9.2Q   Q <u>Problems.</u> During all stops the leader should be alert to any physical or psychological changes in individual group members that may indicate the onset of fatigue, hypothermia, thermal injury, or emotional upset. If symptoms for these problems are observed, the problem should be dealt with immediately.

9.2R   R. <u>Keeping It All Together.</u> During any and all stops the leader should emphasize to the group the need to keep all their equipment together so that nothing is lost or left behind.

CAMP ACTIVITIES AND TECHNIQUES

Objective: To familiarize the leader with activities, skills, and techniques that are best experienced in camp.

Desired Understanding:

1. The leader's role as a teacher in camp.

2. Common activities, skills, and techniques that can be used as learning experiences in camp.

10.1 1. <u>The Leader's Role as a Camp Teacher.</u> As with teaching along the trail, the leader should not overburden the group members with too much information at one time. Teaching should be done systematically and/or when an opportune time or situation presents itself and is conducive to a particular learning experience. This is not to say that the leader should allow unsafe actions to occur, for that unsafe situation is indeed an opportune time for a learning experience.

The leader should not expect every group member to be an expert in every skill technique; rather he or she should allow them to learn what they can through experience, both positive and negative.

10.2 2. <u>Common Activities, Skills and Techniques That Can Be Used as Learning Experiences in Camp.</u>

10.2A A. <u>Choosing a Campsite.</u> "It is human nature to choose a campsite for its aesthetic qualities. This is fine as long as conservation is kept in mind, but beauty is everywhere in the wilds, not just lake shores or river banks, along trails and in other scenic spots" (Petzolt, 1974, p. 110).

1. <u>Safety.</u> Since the major consideration for any backpacking trip should be safety, the leader should help the group members develop the ability to evaluate a potential campsite for safety hazards. What follows is a list of safety criteria used in evaluating a potential campsite:

a. Never camp on top of a cliff face. There is danger from lightning and also that of having someone accidentally fall over the cliff.

b. Never camp at the base of a cliff. There is danger from lightning and also of a possible rockfall.

c. Avoid areas with large dead trees, whose branches may crash to the ground during a high wind.

d. Avoid areas with large exposed root systems. There is danger from tripping.

e. Avoid dry stream beds. There is danger from flash flooding during a heavy rain.

2. Sight and Sound. The leader should emphasize to the group the need to respect the privacy and solitude sought by other campers. Unless the group is obligated to camp at a particular area, they should choose a campsite that is both out of sight and out of sound of other campsites and trails.

3. Choosing the High Ground or the Low Ground. The leader should familiarize the group with the advantage of choosing a campsite located on high ground or low ground. In the summer it is advantageous to camp on high ground to avoid the dampness often found in low areas and to avoid insects that frequent wet damp areas. The high ground will also allow the group to take advantage of any cooling breezes. In the winter, low lying campsites usually provide protection from the wind. The "wind-chill effect" can have very harmful effects on both people and equipment.

4. Availability of Water. Group members should be made aware of proper use of water sources and the rights of others to use these water sources.

Safe drinking water is usually a prerequisite for a good campsite. The actual campsite need not be located extremely close to the water source. By camping some distance away, the chance of polluting the source is reduced and other hikers can have access to the water without having to parade through the group's campsite.

B. <u>Choosing a Location and Constructing a Camp Latrine.</u>
The leader should demonstrate where a camp latrine should be
located and how it should be constructed.

1. <u>Choosing a Location.</u>

   a. The location should be at least 30 yards from the near-
      est trail campsite or water source.

   b. The location should be well hidden to insure privacy
      for the user.

   c. Avoid locations that may present a run-off problem
      during a heavy rain.

2. <u>Construction.</u>

   a. An 8- by 14-inch hole should be dug to a depth of 8 to
      14 inches but not going below the organic level of the
      soil.

   b. All soil removed from the hole should be piled at a
      convenient location for the users to cover wastes in
      the hole after each use.

   c. Heavy fallen branches may be used as supports or as
      seats.

3. <u>Use.</u>

   a. After each use, soil should be sprinkled over the feces
      and the used toilet paper should be burned.

   b. Sanitary napkins or tampons should not be deposited in
      the latrine but carried out in a double plastic bag and
      disposed of in a container where animals cannot get
      at them.

   c. A handkerchief may be tied to a branch on the way to
      the latrine as a notification that the latrine is occupied.

   d. After camp is "broken, " the entire latrine should be
      filled in and relandscaped so that it cannot be seen
      that a latrine was once there.

10.2C C. <u>Preparing a Cooking Area.</u> The leader should demonstrate to the group the proper preparation of a cooking area. If a "fire ring," "fire pit," or "fire place" is in existence at your campsite, use it. If there is no existing facility, there are a few rules to follow in preparing a cooking area.

1. Choose an area well away from tent sites and other areas of heavy traffic.

2. Clear away all combustible ground cover to a distance of five feet in diameter from the location of the stove or fire. After camp is broken, this material should be replaced.

3. A sump hole should be dug for the disposal of wash water and for all unburned coals after the fire is extinguished (Kelsey, 1974).

10.2D D. <u>Tent Sites.</u> The leader should explain to the group the benefits gained from choosing a proper tent site. The following criteria should be used in choosing a proper tent site and in properly positioning a tent.

1. Be conscious of any long-term environmental damage that may occur if a tent is pitched on a particular location. An example of possible long-term damage would be the results of pitching a tent on top of fragile alpine flora that has a slow recovery rate.

2. Try to choose a flat location with deep dry ground cover.

3. Small twigs, branches, and stones may be removed to prevent damage to the tent floor and for the comfort of the occupants. All material removed should be replaced after the tent is taken down.

4. The tent site should be up wind from all fires.

5. The tent should be erected so that the rear of the tent is facing into the wind. This is usually the most wind stable position and it will prevent rain and snow from entering the tents when the occupants enter and exit the tent.

6. <u>Never</u> dig a trench around a tent. It is both unnecessary and environmentally damaging.

10.2E   E.   <u>Personal Hygiene.</u> The leader should make the group members aware of the need for personal hygiene on a backpacking trip and the proper method to wash and bathe without polluting the water source.

Few people enjoy being dirty and smelly and few people enjoy working or even being around someone who is unclean. All group members should try to keep as neat and clean as possible. It is reasonable to assume that most people will get dirty on a backpacking trip. It is not reasonable that a person remain that way if conditions allow that person to wash or bathe. There are few conditions that would prohibit a hiker from brushing his or her teeth or combing his hair.

When washing or bathing, there is a certain procedure to follow that will prevent the polluting of the water source:

1. All washing, whether with or without soap, should be done well away from the water source. This is accomplished by carrying pots full of water to the chosen location.

2. Only after all soap suds are rinsed off the person may he or she take a plunge in the stream or lake for a final rinse.

3. Only biodegradable soap should be used.

10.2F   F.   <u>Swimming.</u> If the group plans to go swimming at any time during the trip, the leader should maintain a high standard of safety. He or she should explain the reasons for these high standards.

1. If "minors" are on the trip, the leader should acquire the parents' permission before the trip to allow their son or daughter to go swimming.

2. The leader should not allow any nonswimmers to go into deep or fast-moving waters.

3. Swimmers should be paired so that everyone always has at least one person looking after him or her.

4. The entire group should swim in the same general location as a safety precaution.

5. If there is a place from which to jump or dive into the water, the depth of the water should be checked to insure that it is deep enough to safely engage in such activities.

10. 2G   G. Good Camping Habits. The leader should help each group member develop good camping habits both for personal safety and the conservation of the environment. What follows is a good sampling of good camping habits the leader may help the group members develop and practice:

1. If any group member wants to leave the general vicinity of the campsite, he or she should make the group leader aware of who are going, where they are going, and when they will be back.

2. If animals present a problem, it may be necessary to put all food in waterproof sacks and hang them from tree branches well out of the reach of all animals.

3. If bears, in particular, are a potential problem, do not allow any food in the tents at any time. A tent is no match for a hungry bear!

4. Females should consider their menstrual cycle when planning a backpacking trip. Women having their period have been attacked by bears.

5. Never cut live trees or plants. The wilderness should remain the way you found it and not be altered in any way.

6. Upon leaving a campsite the leader should inspect the area. It should look natural and as if no one had ever camped there.

CHAPTER 11

POST-TRIP ACTIVITIES

Objective: To familiarize the leader with different post-trip activities.

Desired Understanding:

1. Types of activities to be conducted after the trip.

11.1   1. <u>Types of Activities to Be Conducted Immediately After the Trip.</u>

11.1A   A. <u>Notification.</u> Immediately after the finish of the hike, the leader should contact the person mentioned in section 8. 4C and let him know that the group is out of the woods and all is well. <u>This is mandatory!</u> If the person is not notified, he or she may send for help and much money and manpower will be wasted.

11.1B   B. <u>Trash and Garbage.</u> As soon as possible after the finish of the hike, all trash and garbage carried out should be deposited in an appropriate receptacle.

11.1C   C. <u>Personal Clean-up.</u> If facilities are available, all group members should take a shower or wash up before the trip home. It is also nice to have a clean set of clothes in the vehicle to change into for the trip home.

11.1D   D. <u>Future Meetings.</u> Arrangements should be made for the group to meet to clean and return all group equipment and other equipment that was rented or borrowed. Any extra food left over from the trip can be distributed at this time.

11.1E   E. <u>Evaluation Sheets.</u> Before group members are dropped off at their homes, they should be given an "Evaluation Sheet" which they should fill out and return at some predetermined date. These "Evaluation Sheets" can become excellent references for future trips and can help the leader become aware of his or her strengths and weaknesses. See Appendix S.

11.1F   F. <u>Car Wash.</u> It is a show of thanks to the vehicle owners to have a free car wash conducted by the group for the vehicles that were used on the trip.

11.1G   G. <u>Budget.</u> Within a few days after the trip, the leader should go over the budget and determine if any money is to be collected or returned to the group members or the sponsoring organization. See Appendix T.

CHAPTER 12

BUDGET

Objective: To have the leader become aware of the need to project a budget and the need to maintain a record of all monetary transactions.

12.1   1. When working with a group, it is necessary to record all money transactions. This is usually done by constructing a proposed budget, collecting that money and keeping a record of all money spent. In this way the group will know how much was spent, and it can also act as a resource in planning future trips. There are many considerations in planning a budget.

12.1A   A. How Much? If costs to the sponsoring organization and/or group members are too high, it may be necessary to plan a less costly trip by going somewhere closer or going for a shorter time period.

12.1B   B. Notification. The group members and the sponsoring organization should be made aware of the cost to them, as soon as possible.

12.1C   C. Collections. Many items that need to be or could be paid for prior to the trip can be paid if all money is collected from the group members and the sponsoring organization, by the leader, well in advance of the trip.

12.1D   D. Refunds and Collections. The leader should keep track of all money spent so that refunds or further collections can be made. See Appendix T.

REFERENCES

Fear, E. Outdoor Living: Problems, solutions, guidelines. Tacoma, Washington: Survival Education Association, 1971.

Fear, E. Surviving the unexpected wilderness emergency. Tacoma, Washington: Survival Education Association, 1974.

Goddard, E. A trail profile. Why? How? Cupertino, California: Antelope Camping Equipment, 1975.

Kelsey, R. Walking in the wild. New York: Funk & Wagnalls, 1974.

Manning, H. Backpacking: One step at a time. Seattle, Washington: R.E.I. Press, 1972.

Mitchell, D. Mountaineering first aid. Seattle, Washington: The Mountaineers, 1972.

Pallister, N. NOLS cookery. Emporia, Kansas: Teachers College Press, 1974.

Petzolt, P. Adventure education and the national outdoor leadership school. Journal of Outdoor Education , 1975, 10 (1), 3-7.

Petzolt, P. The wilderness handbook. New York: Norton, 1974.

Van Der Smissen, B. Legal aspects of adventure activities. Journal of Outdoor Education, 1975, 10(1), 12-15.

Walbridge, C. How to handle a heavy pack. Wilderness Camping, 1975, 5(3), 26-28.

Wilkerson, J. (Ed.) Medicine for mountaineering (2nd ed.) Seattle, Washington: The Mountaineers, 1976.

APPENDIX

Reproduction of Forms

Unless otherwise noted, the author grants permission for the purchaser of this book to reproduce all the following appendixes for his or her use as a group leader. These reproductions may be used only for group members under the purchaser's charge and must not be sold.

APPENDIX A

(See pages 32 and 33 of text)

Estimated Hiking Times

TRIP ITINERARY

Name of trip: _____

Purpose of the trip: _____

Location of activity: _____

Location address: _____

                 number   street

_____

              city   state   zip code

Location telephone number in case of emergency _____

                                   area code   number

Dates of activity: from: _____ to: _____

                day, month, date   day, month, date

Departure time: _____

                   day, month, date

Departure location: _____

Departure address: _____

               number   street

_____

              city   state   zip code

Departure location telephone number: _____

                             area code   number

Estimated distance from departure location to activity location: _____

                                           miles

Estimated travel time: _____

               hours   minutes

Estimated time of arrival at activity location: _____

Meal arrangements during travel: _____

_____

_____

Estimated time of departure from activity location: _

                                 time   date

Estimated time of return: _____

                 time   date

Return location: _____

Return address: _____

            number   street

_____

              city   state   zip code

Return location telephone number: _____

                            area code   number

Cost to participant: $ _____

Cancellation refund: _____ %, before _____

                                   time, day, month, date

DAILY ITINERARY

Day #		
Day	Month	Date
Location name		
Map reference		
Wake-up time		
Breakfast time	from	to
Breakfast will be prepared by		
Breakfast will require cooking?	Yes ( )	No ( )
Clean-up time	from	to
"Begin hiking time"		
Trail name		
Type of trail markers followed		
Lunch time	from	to
Lunch prepared by		
Lunch will require cooking?	Yes ( )	No ( )
Location name		
Map reference		
"Begin hiking time"		
Trail name		
Type of trail markers followed		
Arrival time at campsite		
Location name		
Map reference		
Set-up time	from	to
Supper time	from	to
Supper prepared by		
Supper will require cooking?	Yes ( )	No ( )
Clean-up time	from	to

	Day	Trip total
Distance hiked		
Hours hiked		
Elevation gains		
Elevation losses		

(Please print)

Name
Address

Telephone number
Vehicle number
Are you the driver?   Yes ( )   No ( )
Cook group number

Name
Address

Telephone number
Vehicle number
Are you the driver?   Yes ( )   No ( )
Cook group number

Name
Address

Telephone number
Vehicle number
Are you the driver?   Yes ( )   No ( )
Cook group number

Name
Address

Telephone number
Vehicle number
Are you the driver?   Yes ( )   No ( )
Cook group number

APPENDIX E

PARENT PERMISSION SLIP AND MEDICAL RELEASE FORM

We give our child, _____ , permission

to participate in the_____trip on_____

We expect that the teacher-leaders will take reasonable precautions to

insure safety of our child and we absolve_____
                                             leader/leaders
and _____of liability for any accident or illness which
       organization
might occur on this trip. Should it be necessary to incur additional

expenses and/or treatment during the trip, we give the trip leaders

permission to use their judgment in such matters and will reimburse

them for any expenses. We, as parents, have decided (with or without

medical assistance) that our child is physically able to participate

and we acknowledge that any accident insurance we consider necessary

will be our responsibility to locate and purchase.

Signed_____

_____

Date _____

(WARNING: The above form is only an example. Both a physician and
an attorney should be consulted in constructing your own.)

APPENDIX F

WAIVER OF CLAIMS AND RELEASE FROM LIABILITY

The undersigned, in consideration of being permitted to participate in a trip for educational/recreational purposes from _____

city

_____, beginning on_____, 197__,

state

and from said destination returning to_____ , on or

city, state

about_____ , 197__ , does hereby irrevocably, person-

ally and for his or her heirs, assigns and legal representatives release and waive any and all past, present or future claims, demands, and causes of action which the undersigned now has or may in the future have against _____ , _____ ,

leader/leaders   sponsoring organization

its members, representatives, officers, agents, employees, and each of them, for any and all past, present, or future loss of or damage to property and/or bodily injury, including death, however caused, result-ing from, arising out of or in any way connected with the aforementioned trip for educational/recreational purposes on the aforesaid dates.

The undersigned covenants not to cause any action at law or in equity to be brought or permit such to be brought in his or her behalf, either directly or indirectly, on account of loss or of damage to property and/ or bodily injury, including death, against any of the aforesaid parties however caused, resulting from, arising out of or in any way connected with the aforementioned trip, and agrees to save, indemnify, hold harm-less, and defend at his or her sole expense, any and all of the aforesaid parties from any claims, demands, and causes of action which now or in the future be asserted against the aforesaid parties arising out of or by reason of said trip described above, including any incident, injury, loss, or damage that might occur at any place in connection therewith.

The undersigned further states and affirms that he or she is aware of the fact that the aforesaid trip and travel, even under the safest con-ditions possible, may be hazardous; that he or she assumes the risk of any and all loss of or damage to property and/or bodily injury, including death, however caused, resulting from, arising out of or in any way connected with the aforementioned trip; that he or she is of legal age and is competent to sign this Waiver of Claims and Release from Liabi-lity; and that he or she has read and understands all of the provisions herein contained.

The undersigned further states and affirms that he or she, if assuming the responsibility of operating a vehicle on said trip, has a valid operator's permit or license and is adequately covered by insurance, including public liability coverage.

Dated at _____ , _____ , 19___.

Signed:_____

(Warning: The above is only an example. An attorney should be consulted in constructing your own.)

PERSONAL REFERENCE SHEET

Name:_____
School address:_____
School phone no.:_____
Home address:_____
               street   city   state   zip code

Home phone no.:_____

IN CASE OF EMERGENCY, PLEASE NOTIFY:

Name:_____
Address:_____
             street   city   state   zip code
Phone no.:_____
Relationship:_____

OR:

Name:_____
Address:_____
             street   city   state   zip code
Phone no.:_____
Relationship:_____

LIST ALL CHRONIC ILLNESSES, ALLERGIES, OR HANDICAPS:

_____
_____

LIST ALL MEDICATIONS YOU ARE NOW TAKING:

_____
_____

                            Sign:_____

APPENDIX H

MENU PLANNER

DATE	Weight (oz./group)																
	Cost (per group)																
	Cost (per person)																
	Carbohydrate (gm./person)																
	Fat (gm./person)																
	Protein (gm./Person)																
	Calories (gm./person)																
	Weight (oz./person)																
	Carbohydrate (gm./1b.)																
	Fat (gm./1b.)																
DAY	Protein (gm./1b.)																
	Calories (per 1b.)																
MEAL	ITEM																

98

PERSONAL EQUIPMENT LIST

1. ( ) 1 pr. — Hiking boots (well broken in)
2. ( ) 3 pr. — Socks (wool)
3. ( ) 1 pr. — Shorts (baggy)
4. ( ) 1 pr. — Long trousers (light, baggy)
5. ( ) 1 pr. Long trousers (wool, baggy)
6. ( ) 1 — Shirt (light, long sleeve, baggy)
7. ( ) 2 — Shirts or sweaters (wool, long sleeve, baggy)
8. ( ) 2 — Handkerchiefs (large)
9. ( ) 1 Hat (felt, w/brim)
10. ( ) 1 Cap (stocking type)
11. ( ) 1 — Bathing suit
12. ( ) 3 pr. — Underwear
13. ( ) 1 — Poncho, rain suit, or cagoule
14. ( ) 1 — Cook kit (one per every 4 people)
         (1½ qt. pot, 2 qt. pot, fry pan)
15. ( ) 1 Stove (one every 2 people)
16. ( ) 1 1 qt. Fuel bottle and fuel
17. ( ) 1 Funnel (one per every 2 people)
18. ( ) 1 Bowl (unbreakable)
19. ( ) 1 Cup (unbreakable)
20. ( ) 1 Spoon
21. ( ) 1 1 qt. Water bottle (unbreakable)
22. ( ) 1 Waterproof matchcase w/strike anywhere matches
23. ( ) 1 Fire starter (candle, paste, solid)
24. ( ) 1 Sleeping bag
25. ( ) 1 Sleeping pad (open or closed cell foam)
26. ( ) 1 Tent (one per every 2 people)
27. ( ) 1 Personal first aid kit
28. ( ) 50' 1/8" Nylon cord
29. ( ) 1 Flashlight w/new bulb and batteries
30. ( ) 1 Compass
31. ( ) Map/maps and/or guidebooks
32. ( ) 1 Repair kit ("rip-stop" nylon tape, needles, thread,
         stove parts, pack parts, flashlight bulb)
33. ( ) Toilet paper
34. ( ) Insect repellent
35. ( ) 1 Pocket knife
36. ( ) 1 Whistle
37. ( ) 1 Camera and film (optional)
38. ( ) 1 Notebook and pencil
39. ( ) 1 Pack and frame
40. ( ) 1 Toothbrush

P G S APA A

Pv G APA B

41.	( )	1	Small tube of toothpaste
42.	( )		Biodegradable soap₎
43.	( )	1	Comb
44.	( )	1	Tube or bottle of sunscreen
45.	( )		Sanitary napkins or tampons (if applicable)
46.	( )	1 pr.	Sun glasses
47.	( )	1 pr.	Canvas tennis shoes or moccasins

Notes:

   Total weight for items 1 through 47 should not exceed 30 pounds.

   The owner of a particular piece of equipment is solely responsible in the event of theft, loss or damage to that piece of equipment.

APPENDIX J

GROUP EQUIPMENT LIST

1. ( ) 1   Small axe

2. ( ) 1   Folding saw

3. ( ) 1   Small shovel

4. ( ) 1   Repair kit ("rip-stop" nylon tape, needles, thread, pliers, screwdriver, wire, magnifying glass)

5. ( ) 1   5 gal. water carrier

6. ( ) 1   Group first aid kit

Note:

The theft, loss or damage to any piece of group equipment will be the responsibility of the _entire_ group.

APPENDIX K

PERSONAL FIRST AID KIT

Medication:

( )   Salt tablets

( )   Tincture of Zepherin - antiseptic

( )   Aspirin - minor pain relief

( )   "Chap-Stick"

Hardware:

( )   Moleskin or molefoam

( )   Bandaids

( )   Adhesive tape

( )   Gauze roll (plain)

( )   "Ace bandage" (2")

( )   Nail clip

( )   Butterfly bandages

( )   Gauze pads (4" x 4")

( )   First aid booklet

APPENDIX L

GROUP FIRST AID KIT

Medication

( )	Aspirin	- minor pain relief
( )	Ammonia Inhalant	- revive unconscious
( )	Achromycin	- 250 mgm tablets
		- (RX)
		- broad-spectrum antibiotic
( )	Tincture of Zepherin	- antiseptic
( )	Benadryl	- 25 mgm tablets
		- (RX)
		- antihistamine
( )	Chlor-Trimeton	- 4 mgm tablets
		- (RX)
		- antihistamine
( )	Codeine Tablets	- 30 mgm tablets
		- (RX)
		- pain relief
( )	Compazine	- (RX)
		- nausea control
( )	"Chap-Stick"	
( )	Demerol	- 50 or 100 mgm tablets
		- (RX)
		- pain relief
( )	Dramamine	- (RX)
		- motion sickness
( )	Lambswool	
( )	Lomotil	- (RX)
		- anti-diarrhea
( )	Metycaine Ointment	- (RX)
		- eye injury
( )	Ornade Capsules	- (RX)
		- decongestants
( )	Penicillin Tablets	- (RX)
		- antibiotic
( )	Soap, Yellow	- for poison ivy
( )	Soap, Germicidal "Phisohex"	
( )	Salt Tablets	
( )	Simethicone Tablets	- antacid
( )	Vitamin A Ointment	- burns
( )	Zinc Oxide Ointment	- sun block

WARNING: Consult a physician and a pharmacist in obtaining and using the above mentioned medications.

GROUP FIRST AID KIT

HARDWARE

( )   Adhesive Tape - $\frac{1}{2}$" or 1" or 2"
( )   Ace Bandage - 1" or 2" or 3"
( )   Bandaids (assorted sizes)
( )   Butterfly Bandages
( )   Cotton
( )   Gauze Pads (plain) 1" x 1" or 2" x 2" or 4" x 4"
( )   Gauze Pads (vaseline) or
( )   Gauze Pads (Telfa) or
( )   Gauze Roll (plain) - 1" or 3"
( )   Moleskin or Molefoam
( )   Triangle Bandage
( )   Basswood Splints
( )   Single Edge Razor Blade
( )   Safety Pins
( )   Splint (inflatable)
( )   Splint (wire)
( )   Scissors
( )   Snake Bite Kit
( )   Thermometer (oral)
( )   Tweezers
( )   Hemostat
( )   Nail Clip
( )   Sewing Needle
( )   Mirror
( )   First Aid Booklet

APPENDIX   M

DRIVER'S INFORMATION SHEET

Vehicle number:_____
Driver's name:_____
Driver's address:_____
Driver's telephone number:_____
Year, make, and model of vehicle:_____
Insurance company for vehicle:_____
Insurance company address:_____
Insurance company telephone number in case of an accident
Policy number:_____
Coverage for collision, comprehensive, fire and theft:_____

Driver's insurance company for liability:_____
Insurance company address:_____
Insurance company telephone number in case of an accident:_____
Policy number:_____
Coverage for liability:_____

Road service coverage:_____

Maintenance and Safety Equipment Checklist:

( )   Flashlight

( )   Jack and handle

( )   Lug wrench

( )   Road flairs, flashers or reflectors

( )   Serviceable spare tire

( )   Service/Owner's manual

( )   State registration number_____

( )   Insurance information

( )   Road service information

( )   Functional seatbelts

( )   Operational, flashing hazard lights

APPENDIX N

RESPONSE TO A WILDERNESS ACCIDENT

Accidents can happen anywhere and the wilderness is no exception. It is the leader's responsibility to insure that at least two members of the group be knowledgeable in the area of first aid. Further, it is the responsibility of the leader, along with the assistant leader, to take charge of any emergency situation that occurs during an outing. All group members should be taught how to safely and expediently react to a wilderness emergency. What follows is a step-by-step procedure for reacting to a wilderness emergency, regardless of first aid background. It should be learned and practiced by the entire group before an outing.

Step # 1   All group members should be aware of the location, contents and use of the "Group First Aid Kit."

Step # 2   After an accident has occurred, the leader should take charge immediately. If the leader is the victim, the assistant leader should take control of the situation.

Step # 3   The victim should be approached in a safe manner so as to lessen the danger to the helpers and to further reduce potential danger to the victim.

Step # 4   If the victim can be moved without further danger, seek an immediate, safe location.

Step # 5   The leader or most qualified person in first aid should give the victim an immediate, quick examination, primarily to insure the victim is breathing and to inspect for severe bleeding. If necessary administer immediate first aid.

Step # 6   If the leader needs help from other members of the group he/she should not hesitate to call out for help.

Step # 7   Instructions must be given quickly and precisely. Since there are many chores to be done, the leader should incorporate as many group members as possible. This not only makes the operations more expedient, but, by keeping group members busy, any psychological trauma that group members might experience because of the accident are usually avoided.

Step # 8   After the "breathing and/or bleeding first aid" has been administered, the leader should question the victim to determine if he/she is experiencing any other discomforts.

Step # 9   This should be followed by a more complete examination.

Step # 10   The victim should then be treated for shock by keeping his/her warm and restful.

Step # 11   If the victim is conscious and thirsty, he or she may be given warm liquids if there is no sign of internal bleeding.

Step # 12   When all first aid has been administered, some very important decisions have to be made. The leader should consult with the assistant leader for advice and support, but it is the leader who must make the final decisions. Mitchell (1972) cites the following major decisions:

1. Should the victim be allowed to walk under his own power?

2. Can and should the victim be evacuated by the party at hand?

3. Is outside help needed? (The recommendation here is that even for minor injuries, if there is uncertainty as to the victim's condition, party strength and capability, etc., outside help should be notified.

4. Should the victim remain where he or she is until outside help arrives or should the victim be moved a short distance to a more sheltered area?

Step # 13   After the leader has made these decisions he/she should inform the entire group of his/her plans.

Step # 14   The leader should then fill out an Accident Report Form (see Appendix N of this book) in duplicate. It is extremely important that this form be filled out as completely and accurately as possible.

Step # 15   The leader should, at this time, select at least two strong
             group members to go for help if it is necessary. These
             people should take one copy of the "Accident Report Form,"
             a map showing the group's location, car keys if necessary
             and change to make phone calls. All this is in addition to
             their full compliment of gear.

Step # 16   While waiting for help, the group should be kept busy.
             Again, this is to make the group as a whole more comfort-
             able and to relieve any psychological trauma arising from
             their predicament.

Step # 17   Meanwhile, upon reaching the trail head, those sent for help
             should seek help immediately. Here is where the lack of
             change for a phone could prove deadly in respect to wasted
             time in finding help.

Step # 18   When contact is made with the proper officials, the map and
             "Accident Report Form" should be surrendered, along with
             any additional information that might help the rescuers.

Step # 19   From this point on it is best to let the officials conduct the
             rescue operations unless aid is requested.

Step # 20   When help arrives upon the group's location, all possible
             assistance should be given to aid in the evacuation.

Step # 21   After evacuation, it is the leader's decision to abort the
             trip or to continue.

Remember: A wilderness accident response requires sound leadership
             and the full cooperation of every member of the group.

Reference: Mitchell, Dick. Mountaineering First Aid. Seattle,
             Washington: The Mountaineers, 1972. (p. 16).

ACCIDENT REPORT FORM

This form is to be completed in duplicate AT the scene of the accident for each injured member of the party. One form should be sent with those going for help and the other form retained by the leader.

ACCIDENT	Date: Time: AM / / PM / /
LOCATION	Quadrangle: Section:
	Exact Location (include marked map):
	Terrain: Glacier / / Snow / / Brush / / Timber / /
	Rock / / Trail / / Heather / / Easy / /
	Moderate / / Steep / / Other:
COMPLETE DESCRIPTION OF ACCIDENT	Ascending / / Descending / /
	Roped / / Unroped / /
	Rock Fall / / Ice Fall / /
	Avalanche / / Illness / /
	Excess Heat / / Cold / /
	Equipment Failure / /
	Witnesses: Other:
INJURED PERSON	Name: Age:
	Address: Male / / Female / /
	Phone:
	Whom to Notify: Relation: Phone:
OVERALL CONDITION	Good / / Fair / / Serious / / Fatal / /
	Unconscious: / / No / /
	If yes, length of time:
INJURIES	Injury 1 -- Location on Body: Type of Injury:
	Injury 2 -- Location on Body: Type of Injury:
	Other Location on Body:
	Injuries -- Type of Injury:
	General: Bleeding stopped / / Shelter Built / /
	Artificial Respiration / / Warm Fluids Given / /
	Treated for Shock / / Evacuation / /
FIRST AID TREATMENT	Injury 1
	Injury 2
	Other
	Injuries:
ON THE SCENE PLANS	Will stay put / / Will evacuate to trail / / to Road / /
	Will evacuate a short distance to shelter / /
	Will send some members out / /
	Other:
PERSONNEL	Number: View Finders / / Experienced / / Intermediate / /
	Advanced / / Capability for a bivouac:
	Yes / / No / /

(continued)

	ATTACH the pre-trip prepared LIST OF PARTY MEMBERS including names, addresses and phone numbers to the ACCIDENT FORM BEING TAKEN OUT.
EQUIPMENT AVAILABLE	Tents / / Sleeping Bags / / Ensolite / / Flares / / Saw / / Hardware / / Stove and Fuel / / Ropes / / Other:
WEATHER	Warm / / Moderate / / Freezing / / Snow / / Wind / / Sun / / Clouds / / Fog / / Rain / / Other:
TYPE OF EVACUATION RECOMMENDED	Lowering Operation / / Carry-out / / Helicopter / / Rigid stretcher / / None until specialized medical assistance / / Specify:
PARTY LEADER	Name:
MESSENGERS SENT FOR HELP	Names:
FURTHER INFORMATION, IF ANY	
RECOMMEN- DATIONS FOR FUTURE CLIMBS	Equipment: Leadership: Route: Abilities:

APPENDIX P

HYPOTHERMIA *

<u>Hypothermia</u> is a condition which results from the body's inability to produce heat faster than it loses it. As the temperature of the core of the body drops, breakdown of physical and mental functioning takes place. Death is the end result unless remedied by increasing that core temperature.

Hypothermia (exposure) is a major killer of outdoorsmen each year. It can and does occur at temperatures well above "freezing" (32° F) if one or more "Predisposing Factors" (see accompanying chart) are present. All group members should be acquainted with these factors plus the symptoms, prevention and treatment of hypothermia. Group leaders intending to lead a group in an area where the threat of hypothermia exists should research all aspects of this life threatening condition.

*Note: The following material may not be reproduced without the consent of the copyright holder. Parts of this appendix are from Hypothermia: <u>Killer of the Unprepared</u> by Theodore G. Lathrop, M.D., Portland, Oregon: The Mazamas, 1975. Copyright 1973 by the Mazamas.

ACCIDENTAL HYPOTHERMIA

PREDISPOSING FACTORS

- Poor condition
- Inadequate nutrition and hydration
- Thin build
- Non-woolen clothing
- Inadequate protection from wind, rain, snow
- Getting wet
- Exhaustion

SIGNS (observed by others)

- Poor coordination
- Slowing of pace
- Stumbling
- Thickness of speech
- Amnesia
- Irrationality, poor judgment
- Hallucinations
- Loss of contact with environment
- Blueness or puffiness of skin
- Dilation of pupils
- Decreased heart and respiratory rate
- Weak or irregular pulse
- Stupor

SYMPTOMS (felt by self)

- Intense shivering
- Muscle tensing
- Fatigue
- Feeling of deep cold or numbness
- Poor coordination
- Stumbling
- Poor articulation (thickness of speech)
- Disorientation
- Decrease in shivering, followed by rigidity of muscles
- Blueness or puffiness of skin
- Slow, irregular or weak pulse

PREVENTION

- Good rest and nutrition prior to climb
- Continued intake of food
- Waterproof-windproof clothing (some woolen)
- Emergency bivouac equipment
- Early bivouac in storm or if lost or be-nighted
- Exercise to keep up body's heat production (isometric contraction of muscles)

TREATMENT

REDUCE HEAT LOSS:

- Shelter the victim from wind and weather
- Insulate him from the ground
- Replace wet clothing with dry
- Put on windproof, waterproof gear
- Increase exercise level if possible

ADD HEAT:

- Hot drinks
- Put in warmed sleeping bag (with another person)
- Heat from hot stones or hot canteen of water
- Huddle for body heat from others
- Immerse in tub of hot water (110°F)

Hypothermia: Killer of the Unprepared by Theodore G. Lathrop, M.D.

APPENDIX Q

FROSTBITE *

<u>Superficial Frostbite</u> or "frost-nip" is an injury to the skin and immediate underlying tissue instigated by extreme cold and the body's inability to adequately heat that portion of the body. Extremities such as toes, fingers, noses, and ears are usually the most vulnerable areas.

<u>Deep Frostbite</u> is a continuation of "superficial frostbite" usually resulting in damage to deeper layers of tissue and, at times, damage or destruction to bone and muscle.

Frostbite begins when ice crystals form between tissue cells. As the ice crystals grow, water is drawn from the cells. This creates a biochemical reaction, killing the cells and permanently damaging the tissues. This is further complicated by the freezing and clotting of small arteries and veins which lose their ability to bring heat to the injured area.

Symptoms

Before frostbite actually begins the vulnerable area will appear red and puffy. The area will usually ache from pain caused by the extreme cold. If unchecked the area will become numb and the pain will diminish.

Superficial Frostbite

1. White or yellowish white skin color of the injured area.

2. When pressed with a finger the skin surface feels hard: however, the underlying tissue remains soft and resilient.

Deep Frostbite

1. White or yellowish white skin color of the injured area with a waxy appearance.

2. When pressed with a finger the skin surface and all underlying tissue feels hard and wooden-like.

* Note: The following material may not be reproduced without the consent of the copyright holder. Parts of this appendix are

113

from Frostbite: What It Is, How To Prevent It, Emergency Treatment by Bradford Washburn. Boston, Massachusetts: Museum of Science, Boston, 1963. Copyright 1963 by Museum of Science, Boston.

(Washburn, 1963)

Prevention

Overall physical well-being, good clothing and intelligent operations in the field are by far the best insurance against frostbite. When you are exhausted, hungry, ill, injured or hypoxic, your chances of frostbite injury are increased. A few basic tips for prevention follow:

1. Dress intelligently to maintain general body warmth. In cold, windy weather, don't forget to protect your face, head and neck adequately. Enormous amounts of body heat can be lost through these often neglected parts of the body, despite ample protection everywhere else.

2. Eat plenty of the right sort of appetizing food to produce maximum output of body heat. Diet in cold weather at low altitude should tend heavily toward fats, with carbohydrates next and proteins least important. As altitude increases above 10,000 feet, carbohydrates are most important and proteins least. Experiment with fats. If members of the party digest them readily, they are excellent, but don't count on everyone liking them at high altitude.

3. Don't climb under too extreme weather conditions, particularly at high altitudes on exposed terrain. Don't get too early a start in cold weather. Use the configuration of the mountain to help you find maximum shelter and maximum warmth from the sun. In short, use your head--and use it more and more the higher you climb!

4. Avoid all tight, snug-fitting clothing -- particularly on the hands and feet. Socks and boots should fit snugly, with no points of tightness. In putting on socks and boots, carefully eliminate all wrinkles in socks. Don't use old matted insoles.

5. Avoid perspiration under conditions of extreme cold. Wear clothing which ventilates adequately. If you still perspire, remove some of your clothing or slow down! Keep your feet and hands dry. Even with vapor barrier boots, you must not permit your socks to get too wet. All types of boots must be used with great care during periods of inactivity, after exercise has resulted in damp socks or insoles.

114

6.   Wear mittens instead of gloves in extreme cold, except for specialized work like photography or surveying, where great manual dexterity is required for short intervals of time. In these situations, wear a mitten on one hand and a glove temporarily on the other, if possible. If bare-finger dexterity is required, use silk or rayon gloves or cover with adhesive tape all metal parts which must be touched frequently. Remove thumbs and hold fists in palm of mittens occasionally to regain warmth of whole hand.

7.   Always be careful while loading cameras, taking pictures or handling stoves and fuel. Remember that the freezing-point of gasoline is near -70° F., and its rapid rate of evaporation as well as its extreme chill make it very dangerous. Never touch metal objects with bare hands in extreme cold--or even in moderate cold when the hands are moist.

8.   Mitton-shells and gloves to be worn in extreme cold should always be made of soft, flexible dry-tanned deerskin, moose, elk or caribou--not horse-hide, which dries out very stiff after wetting. Removable mitten inserts or glove-linings should be of soft wool. Never use oiled or greased leather gloves, boots or clothing in cold-weather operations. Under many conditions it is wise to tie mittens together on a string hung around your neck or to tie them to the ends of your parka sleeves.

9.   Always carry extra socks, insoles and mittens in your pack.

10.   Keep socks clean--at least those which are worn next to the skin. The use of light, smooth, clean socks next to the skin, followed by one or two heavier outer pairs is good practice.

11.   Keep toenails and fingernails trimmed to reasonable length.
12.   Don't wash your hands, face or feet too thoroughly or too frequently when living under rough-weather conditions. Tough, weather-beaten face and hands, kept reasonable clean, resist frostbite most effectively.

13.   Constant use of wet socks in any type of boot will soften your feet, make the skin more tender, greatly lower resistance to cold and simultaneously increase the danger of other foot-injury such as blistering.

14.   Wind and high altitude should always be approached with respect. Either of them makes otherwise moderate conditions more dangerous. Both together can produce dramatic results when combined with cold.

15.   Don't exercise too strenuously in extreme cold--particularly at high altitude where undue exertion results in panting or very deep breathing. Very cold air brought too rapidly into the lungs will chill your whole body, and under extreme conditions may even damage lung tissues and cause internal hemorrhage.

16.   Once you have been thoroughly chilled (without any injury whatever), it takes several hours of warmth and rest to return your body to normal, regardless of superficial feelings of comfort. When recovering from an emergency cold situation, do not venture out again into extreme cold too soon.

17.   Do not smoke or use alcohol, even in moderation, at high altitude. Never use either tobacco or alcohol at any altitude under conditions when the danger of frostbite is present or after it has occurred.

18.   If you have ever been frostbitten, great care must be taken to protect the once-injured area from future damage.

19.   Much outdoor work in really cold weather cannot possibly be performed in warmth and comfort. Learn carefully how cold you can get while still working safely--then never exceed this limit.

20.   If you are frostbitten or otherwise injured in the field, keep calm; panic or fear will result in perspiration, which in turn will evaporate, causing further chilling which will intensify the crisis and aggravate the injury itself.

21.   Always keep your tetanus boosters up to date. They may give you valuable added protection in the event of frostbite or any other injury in the field.

Treatment

Superficial frostbite can and should be treated immediately. This involves rewarming of the injured area. The following is a brief list of the more common methods of treating superficial frostbite in the field:

1.   For nose, ears, and cheeks: cover the injured area with a warm hand.

2.   For fingers: place the injured fingers in a warm arm pit or crotch.

3. For toes and feet: remove boots and socks from the victim and place the injured feet on a warm chest or in warm armpits. This treatment is a true sign of friendship on the part of the person subjecting his/her bare chest to such cruelties.

The treated areas should be protected from refreezing. If the victim suffers from severe pain, a pain relieving drug may be administered if there is no threat of hypothermia or shock occurring from the side effects of the drug. Should blistering occur, do not treat the injured area any further; rather, abort the trip and seek medical help as soon as possible. Important: Do not rub the injured area.

Deep frostbite should not be treated in the field. If this condition is diagnosed, immediately abort the trip and seek medical help. The treatment calls for rapid rewarming of the injured area, usually resulting in severe pain and possible shock. It is better to have the victim walk out to help than to have him/her suffer the trauma of the pain or the possible physical and psychological trauma of having to be carried out.

APPENDIX R

THERMAL INJURIES *

MAN IN THE HOT ENVIRONMENT

Radiation of heat from the sun has changed nearly one-fifth of the world into arid, desert-like areas, where the heat is so intense that little grows or lives. What little rain does fall to earth in these areas is quickly evaporated, runs off, or sinks deep, leaving the surface inhospitable to man, beast, or vegetation.

The term desert has many connotations. To some it is all sand; to others it's rock, salt or gravel wasteland. Deserts come in all shapes and can be rugged landscapes, rough, gullied or mountainous. Whatever the terrain, it is a place that often has extremes of temperature every day, from very cold at night to very, very hot during the sunlight hours. At times some of these areas can be beautiful and full of color. Then again, they can become a roaring wind or sandstorm which tears everything in its path.

Millions of people have learned how to live in hot environments. They know they must respect the heat and the power of the sun. They know the dangers, and they adjust their lives to meet its daily challenge.

A stranger to this land can adapt and can live in harmony with heat if he/she is aware of the dangers and knows the physiological responses to heat that will take place in the body and knows how to prevent their destructive onslaught.

Regardless of where a person is, hot environments have a detrimental effect on mind, body, and equipment. This does not necessarily have to occur on a desert. It can be in a valley of still air, where the temperature rises because of the lack of air movement; or on the reflected snow on the south face of a mountain. Even the reflected heat of concrete streets and buildings of the big cities can cause a localized very hot environment. Too much heat in any form can quickly upset the delicate balance of a person's inner core temperature and even cause death.

Effects of Heat on the Human Body

The chemical and physical processes that constitute life are very susceptible to the effect of temperature. If the temperature of the tissue in which they operate changes by only a couple of degrees, they tend to get out of balance. As with cold, the regulatory processes called into play to maintain heat balance can set up consequential disturbances which often compound the problem. The first corrective action is for the heart to pump more blood to the blood vessels out near the surface of the skin. Here the sensory nerves dilate the blood vessels and let the too-warm blood circulate close to the skin's cooler surface. This cools the blood by radiation, conduction and convection -- but only as long as the air temperature is cooler than body temperature.

This first stage of body heat reduction is continuous as long as the inner core temperature remains high. When part of the blood fluid is set aside by extreme dilation of the skin blood vessels, and the blood is not being pushed back to the heart, it will threaten the volume-capacity ratio of the body's closed circulatory system. The heart may beat faster, but if the blood is not returning in sufficient quantity, it cannot function properly. This one physiological reaction, if prolonged, can upset the whole body and threaten the most vital organs.

Dilation of the surface blood vessels also increases the leakage of fluids from the capillary blood vessels, causing more blood volume loss from a supply that is already inadequate. This imbalance of volume-capacity ratio in the blood circulatory system appears to be the prime cause of heat exhaustion.

Whenever the inner body temperature rises above 90°, the heat regulatory system calls for insensible or sensible perspiration to cool the skin with water. Insensible perspiration occurs automatically when a minor temperature rise triggers the heat regulatory center. It is called insensible because it is water diffusing through the skin and evaporating before it becomes visible.

Sensible perspiration occurs whenever the body temperature continues to increase, causing the heat regulatory nerve center to open the millions of tiny sweat glands which perforate the skin. The sweat glands can secrete large amounts of water (and heat) upon the skin to be evaporated. Sweating, alone, does little to cool the body, unless the humidity is low enough to assure that the water is evaporated. High relative humidity retards evaporation.

If you experience a high air temperature (above 90°) and high relative humidity (above 75%), your body will be doing everything possible just to hold the optimum body temperature of 99°. This cannot go on indefinitely. Your heart is pumping fast and having trouble getting enough blood to pump, because of all the blood stored in the surface blood vessels. The sweat glands are pouring perspiration (water) and essential chemicals (salt) onto the skin from a limited supply. And if you are working muscles, you are producing still more heat. While the body temperature rises, the metabolic rate, itself, is increased; waste products increase, and the nervous system is disturbed.

To be able to live where extremely high temperatures can be expected, one must first recognize just how serious the local heat problem is and plan to adjust one's activity to lessen the load of heat production and absorption. Then plan and prepare to do everything possible to keep the body temperature from rising further.

Environmental heat affects everyone differently, and the severity increases with age. The degree of heat that would cause heat cramps in a 16-year old may cause heat exhaustion in a person of 40 and heat stroke in those over 60. Generally, the real thermal problem has to do with the reduction or collapse of the body's ability to dissipate heat by circulatory changes and sweating, or a chemical (salt) imbalance caused from too much sweating. This allows the inner core temperature to rise to critical levels.

Knowing the basic effect of heat, one should prepare to counteract its action before it becomes destructive. It can disable the stranger to heat in less than two hours.

Heat That Kills the Unprepared

Outdoor people who travel into hot environments, such as deserts or arid areas, have to plan for the worst. Being aware of the problems is not enough -- one has to be prepared to provide water, shade and body protection, and all of life's necessities. Most hot, arid regions do not have water or ready shade.

Radiated Heat: The sun can make metal, rocks and sand 30° hotter than the air -- hot enough to fry eggs on. And if it can fry eggs, it can burn flesh. Just walking or lying on hot ground or among hot rocks causes the body to gain heat. Touching any metal can burn the hands.

The sun's ultraviolet radiation can burn exposed skin (even tanned skin) and the burn will retard sweating. So remain completely covered with lightweight clothing that reflects heat and sunlight. Wear a head and neck shade. Don't fry the brain -- it's your best survival tool, and your life will depend upon sound decisions now.

In some areas a person can last only a few hours in the direct sun. If you have shade shelter, stay there. If you don't have shade, make some.

Shading the head, and especially the back of the neck, appears to be extremely critical because of the close proximity to that part of the brain which contains a vital nerve center for the control of breathing and circulation. The sides of the neck have several high volume arteries close to the surface, which supply 20% of the body's entire blood flow to the brain. If the neck's skin surface is absorbing abnormal quantities of radiant heat, this may heat the blood and the brain to the critical level and possibly cause sun stroke or heat stroke.

Don't travel during the very high heat of the day. Your problem is keeping the body temperature from rising above 99°, which is not easy when the ground around you is 125°. Wait till the sun is lower on the horizon. Waiting is hard to do when you know loved ones are worrying. But waiting in the shade is the only way to survive long enough to return to them. Waiting a few hours can often make a difficult task easier and safer, or allow the storm to pass.

Heat can cause such a drastic upset of the physiological processes within the body that a person just hasn't the desire to do much of anything. Although anxiety about the situation can override this, persons have been known to die while digging their stuck car out of the sand. Lost persons have pushed on and on till they dropped from the heat.

What To Do to Beat the Heat

You know the blood volume-blood capacity will be threatened by loss of blood due to dilation of skin blood vessels. You know that the heart is having a serious problem getting enough blood to pump. You can help this by slowing down muscle activity and cooling the body any way you can: Shade, fanning, wetting the skin, lessen the demand on the heart.

If you are perspiring this gives you a clue that you are dehydrating, or losing water and salt, both of which are necessary for the body to function. Dangers of dehydration are shown in Figure 1.

If you have water, drink it whenever you are thirsty. Conserve what water you have in your body. Keep lightweight clothing on. Clothes retain the sweat and reduce loss by evaporation. Take salt in small amounts, but only as long as you have water to drink with it. You may feel more comfortable without clothes on in the heat, because your sweat evaporates faster. But you will lose more water -- and without body covering, sunburn of the bare skin can compound your problem.

Desert areas are the most common, but not the only places, for an outdoor person to find too much heat. Heat could challenge ability to stay alive long enough for assistance to arrive or for him or her to improvise life-sustaining needs.

The increase in body temperature can occur in many ways. For instance, a person hiking uphill in heavy clothing can perspire enough water and salt from his or her body to cause dehydration and heat cramps -- and if in the direct sun with little air movement, this can develop into heat exhaustion or heat stroke very quickly. The first symptoms are so vague that people often disregard heat problems in favor of other problems, such as fatigue, being out-of-condition, heavy load, indigestion, headache, nervous tension, etc. People on salt-free diets or those who have failed to drink enough water in the deep canyons or the big cities, can experience heat problems, ignoring the first symptoms or mistaking them for indigestion or nervous tension or hangover.

Heat cramps often impair hikers who forget to replenish salt lost by sweating on a steep trail. Heat cramps are caused by loss of salts from blood and tissue due to excessive sweating.

Activities in the Heat

When the temperature rises, most people slow down. Lack of desire for muscle activity is probably caused by the disturbances in the blood flow, and it could be an automatic process to lessen the chance of more heat load due to muscle heat production. Whatever the reason for slowing down activities, it helps to cool the body.

Water, metal, buildings, concrete, snow, rocks, salt flats, white sand, and anything which will reflect sunlight or retain heat from direct sunlight, can cause local hot spots. Be wary of such areas, or prepare in advance for intense heat.

A person should not attempt any activity that will cause more heat production or body temperature increase. If a person absolutely must work, he should work a few minutes then rest in the shade. Time spent in construction of shade for the work area would be well spent. If perspiring heavily, drink water. Cool the body any way possible.

Play or enjoyment ceases whenever the inner body becomes too warm by only a few degrees or when the water and salt supply becomes low. If the conditions persist and are not reversed, enjoyment not only disappears but a person quickly becomes helpless and unable to take preventive or corrective action.

Emergencies in Hot Environments

Most emergencies will be only of one or two days' duration, and travelers can live through them provided they try to help themselves and do the right things first.

Stay out of direct sun. Improvise body protection (shade).

Slow down all body heat production.

Signal your distress. Colored flags -- clothing -- panels -- smoke -- mirrors. Do everything possible to make yourself more conspicuous and easier to be seen.

Conserve your water: Don't sweat -- and retain the sweat in light clothing. Try not to urinate. Drink water when thirsty. Don't die with water in your canteen.

Foods like proteins increase metabolic heat production and increase water loss. When faced with a short-term heat emergency, food is not necessary for life, but water is. So don't eat. It will only make you thirsty and dry you out.

Don't fight the elements. Stay put under shelter. If caught afoot in a sandstorm, stop traveling. Mark your direction of travel with any- thing available, then lie down with your back to the wind and rest. Cover the face with a cloth. It may be uncomfortable, but it's the only way to stay alive.

Digging a vehicle out of the sand during the hot part of the day in di- rect sunlight may be your last effort. Resting in the shade and delaying the project until later in the day, when it is cooler, may allow you to get home alive.

However, modern people who are strangers in hot, barren, uncivilized environments, often take a dim view of waiting even a short time in this forsaken place and sometimes their imagination is filled with visions of dried bones. Fears can overpower good judgment, replacing it with a determination to escape. Desert rescue teams say that many fatalities are caused by people attempting to walk back from a short outing into the desert, where their vehicle has become stuck in the sand or has developed mechanical problems.

Almost any vehicle can get you so far away from civilization in a few minutes that you cannot walk back alive.

Whenever the sunshine is direct or reflected, expect problems. Whenever the ground is powder dry and devoid of greenery, expect heat problems. Whenever the area has no moving air or wind, expect the heat to rise quickly.

Hazards to Health During Heat Emergencies

Sunburn: Exposure to the direct sun is always dangerous -- it can cause burns that are painful or even fatal. Sunburn is caused by overexposure to ultraviolet radiation. Treat by cooling the skin, applying approved burn medications, and avoiding further exposure.

Sunblindness: Caused by direct or reflected sunlight. Symptoms are burning, watery or inflamed eyes, headaches, and poor vision. The best treatment is prevention, but once sunblinded, protect the eyes from all light and relieve pain. Wear a lightproof bandage and bathe the eyes frequently with cold, wet compresses. Generally the victim will recover in 18 to 20 hours sufficiently to travel with dark glasses.

Exposure to extremely high temperature, high humidity, and direct sunlight may cause four types of heat problems: heat weakness, heat cramps, heat exhaustion, and heat stroke or sun stroke.

Heat weakness: Generally caused by excessively hot, humid environment. Symptoms are easy fatigue, headache, mental and physical inefficiency, poor appetite, insomnia, heavy sweating, high pulse rate, and general physical weakness or loss of strength. Treatment is to drink plenty of water, get to cooler environment, replenish salt loss.

Heat cramps: Usually are caused by strenuous activity in high heat and humidity, where heavy sweating depletes salt level in the blood and tissues.   Symptoms are cramps in the legs and abdominal wall or painful spasms of voluntary muscles. Pupils of the eyes dilate with each spasm. There may be heavy sweating; skin becomes cold and clammy. Unlike stomach aches or abdominal disease symptoms, heat cramps are intermittent. Treatment: Keep the patient resting; give him salt dissolved in water -- but only if plenty of water is available. Often water alone will precipitate the problem; salt deficiency is the primary cause.

Heat exhaustion: Usually is caused by physical exertion during prolonged exposure to heat, which precipitates the overall breakdown of the heat regulatory system and disrupts the circulatory system, causing insufficient supply of blood.

Symptoms: A person is first weak and may have heat cramps, while sweating heavily. The skin is moist and cool, with inner body temperature near normal. The face will be flushed, then pale, with pulse thready and blood pressure low. The victim may vomit or become delirious.

Treatment: Place the person in the shade, flat on his or her back. Give salt with plenty of water. Since the person is cold, keep him or her wrapped up and even give hot drinks, if available. Severe cases may be very serious. If no response to first aid, seek medical help immediately.

Heat stroke and sun stroke: These are caused by a failure of the heat regulatory system which causes the automatic process of body cooling by sweating to stop. This is serious because when the automatic cooling stops, the inner body temperature can quickly rise to over $106°$. Heat stroke is brought on by excessive sweating under conditions of high heat, high humidity, radiation absorption, or muscle activity in a windless environment, where the thermoregulatory system is being overworked. Advanced age or illness can be contributing factors.

Symptoms: Weakness, nausea, headache, heat cramps and even mild heat exhaustion. Body temperature will rise rapidly, pulse will be pounding, and blood pressure is high. Delirium or coma is common. Sweating will stop just before heat stroke becomes apparent. Armpits will be dry. Skin is first flushed and pink, then turning to ashen or purple in later stages.

Treatment: This is a serious medical emergency. Move to a cooler environment and cool the body any way possible. Get medical assistance fast. The internal automatic heat regulatory system is out of balance and has stopped functioning. Body temperature must be regulated artificially from outside the body until the heat regulatory system can be rebalanced.

Any of these hazards to health can occur anywhere and any time the environmental temperature and humidity increase simultaneously. The problem may occur anywhere or any time a person can become overheated by physical exercise or sweat profusely.

Water Requirements of the Human Body

Water in the body and on the body provides the most effective coolant to control the inner body temperature. But it also may be the most limited coolant available to the outdoor person in a desert situation. Water is the third requirement of life -- succeeded only by air and body shelter. The human body is approximately 80% water. Intake and output of liquids are necessary to the processes of life and the normal functions of the vital organs. When water loss exceeds intake, dehydration takes place. Avoid alcohol in any form, as it accelerates dehydration.

Humans lose water three ways: perspiration, respiration and urination. The first two are the automatic processes that remove excess body heat from the body. Urination removes the waste products of food oxidation and muscle or energy use. There is little a person can do about these automatic water losses, but it is useful to know their insidious effects. Losing water to the extent of $2\frac{1}{2}\%$ of body weight, or approximately $1\frac{1}{2}$ quarts of body water, will reduce his or her efficiency 25%. If a person is working, walking or playing in a temperature of 110°, normal ability will be reduced another 25%. The sweat rate of one hiking in hot conditions can increase to two quarts per hour.

Reduced ability quickly becomes a critical factor in desert emergencies, where water and salt resupply are limited. Dehydration symptoms are shown in Figure 1.

SIGNS AND SYMPTOMS OF DEHYDRATION IN MAN

AT VARIOUS DEFICITS OF BODY WATER

1%-5% of body weight	6%-10% of body weight	11%-20% of body weight
Thirst	Dizziness	Delirium
Vague discomfort	Headache	Spasticity
Economy of movement	Labored breathing	Swollen tongue
No appetite	Tingling in limbs	Inability to swallow
Flushed skin	Decreased blood	Deafness
Impatience	volume	Dim vision
Sleepiness	Increased blood	Shriveled skin
Increased pulse rate	concentration	Painful urination
Increased rectal	Absence of salivation	Numb skin
temperature	Cyanosis (blue body)	
Nausea	Indistinct speech	
	Inability to walk	

Figure 1

To an outdoor person, the first warning of serious dehydration is the color of urine. A dark yellow indicates that the body is short of water. Thirst is easily suppressed, and a person desperately in need of water physiologically need not feel unduly thirsty. For this reason, all survival manuals urge that you drink your water as you feel thirsty. Do not hoard water.

The optimum ways to conserve body water are to lessen the heat load -- slow down activity. Rest in shade, hike in shade of canyon walls -- keep clothing on. Keep mouth shut. Get up off the hot ground (it can be 30 $^\circ$ cooler a foot above the ground.)

In any hot environment, drinking plenty of water and replenishing salt losses are the requirements for staying physically healthy. But in the desert your life depends on your water supply.

APPENDIX S

FATIGUE, FEAR AND OTHER PSYCHOLOGICAL PROBLEMS*

"Fatigue" is a term of many meanings, but is basically used to describe those changes of performance that take place over a period of time during which some part of the bodily mechanism gets overloaded. This could be sensory, control, or muscular.

Muscle fatigue is understandable to the outdoor person who depends upon his or her arms, feet, legs and back to carry the body and its necessities in quest of adventure. All too often these muscles are overworked by attempting to travel too far too fast. Tolerable muscle fatigue is good for the total body. It thrives on work. It uses work to improve the cardio-vascular system and respiration, to strengthen muscles, and in general to improve itself.

Only when we travel past the fatigue stage toward the exhaustion stage does it become dangerous to life. In the exhaustion stage the body has a surplus of detrimental waste products and a serious deficit of available and usable energy. Without energy the body's automatic functions deteriorate, threatening the total body.

Most of you reading this book have experienced muscle fatigue at some time during your lives. You have probably experienced other types of fatigue, although the cause may not be quite so obvious.

Mental fatigue causes inattention, carelessness, loss of judgment and reasoning.

Emotional fatigue causes deterioration of normal habits and attitudes.

*Note: The following material may not be reproduced without the consent of the copyright holders:

From Outdoor Living: Problems, Solutions, Guidelines by E. Fear (Ed.). Tacoma, Washington: Survival Education Association, 1971/72. Copyright 1971 by Survival Education Association.

From Surviving the Unexpected Wilderness Emergency (Rev. ed.) by E. Fear. Tacoma, Washington: Survival Education Association, 1973. Copyright 1973 by E. Fear.

Sensory fatigue causes disruption of the senses of hot, cold, alertness to danger, etc.

Mental fatigue in outdoors people generally results from the monotony of uninteresting travel or confinement because of weather. How do you combat the drudgery of following the seemingly endless footprints in the snow, sand, or "tunnel trail" through high trees? Conquering a summit gives the mind excitement. False summits, fought for at the expense of chronic fatigue and determination, are mentally demoralizing in the light of reality. Nothing seems to demoralize a group quicker than inability to actually see the goal, as in the case of fog, clouds, false summits, or forest. This is one reason being lost is so terrifying. The lost person has lost sight of all goals -- the route, the destination, the direction to security, i.e., home, car or camp.

Emotional fatigue is the other mental stress outdoor people should consider whenever in group activity. Some people travel too fast, others travel too slow. Each wishes to travel in his or her personal comfort zone. Each wants the other to change his or her pace. Eventually the unhappy ones vent their feelings. Forced travel in uninteresting environments, such as the "I'll go if you do" person, or the child that is cajoled into a hike with someone else can be frustrating, disappointing, and lacking in rewards for all participants. Each suffers emotional fatigue that could jeopardize the party's behavior, attitude, and the outcome of the journey. When a small group is traveling together, little things become big things very rapidly. Emotions become tense because of exasperation for the stupidity of others. Mistakes will happen. People are different; they have different attitudes, values, habits. Personality and behavioral patterns must be compensated for by the group.

The emotional state of the body is also important because love, hate, and fear affect immediate habits, attitudes and motivation, which may affect the body's mental and physical state. Whenever someone is forced out of his or her personal zone of comfortable actions, he or she develops a fear of the unknown. Imaginations of failure or embarrassment will cause hesitation or stagefright in the person who is suddenly called upon for performance outside of his accustomed activities.

Everyone has a comfort zone. Some people are leaders, others are followers. Some are players, some are watchers. Whenever an emergency suddenly transfers someone out of his or her comfort zone, it causes emotional stress.

Sensory fatigue: Some modern people are attuned to noise. Without it they become uneasy. To others, silence is the blessing they search for. However, the steady noise of the incessant wind, roar of big engines, high pitched tone of a whistle, wear on the sensory nerves. Such fatigue affects attitude, habits, and personal values.

To the autoist it may only be center line focus or the monotony of miles of straight road that dulls the senses and slows the body's motor nerve reactors. Hunters, searching for the elusive deer, begin to see horns where no horns are. Their senses become overburdened and the determination and desire increases the time grows short, until they see horns on anything that moves.

Numbness of skin or fatigue within the extremities of the nerve system disrupts the body's warning and defense mechanisms. Without the feeling and sensory reactions to heat and cold, we may burn hands on hot pots or freeze flesh without realizing it.

Survival is approximately 100% mental because the mind controls the body, its actions and reasoning. Since it is so powerful, we must understand and recognize the conscious level dangers and even consider some of the unusual functions of the subconscious mind.

The Bible says, "As he thinketh in his heart, so is he." The truth in those few words is evident every day. If a person says he or she feels lousy -- he or she will. If a person says he or she feels great -- chances are he or she will -- all day. The same applies to any given task. If you think it will fizzle, it will. If you are convinced you can do it, more often than not you will succeed.

Some call it positive thinking. Some call it "can do" attitude. Whatever it is called, you must have it to survive all alone. You will act only as you see your self-image at that moment. If you see your self-image as strong, you will be strong. If you think yourself a weakling, you will be weak. If you think you can't do it, you probably won't do it. If you think you can't survive, you won't try to survive.

Positive thinking is an indispensable asset in improving a difficult situation. It should not be attempted as a substitute for good judgment in selecting a goal.

The subconscious mind is always the mirror of your self-image. It gets its thought fuel from your values, habits and attitude. The subconscious mind is always working and always open for suggestions. Tell a friend that he or she looks as if he or she has a cold, and chances are

130

the symptoms will develop. Tell someone that a minor cut will hurt badly, it probably will hurt more than before.

This is nothing new. The Orientals knew about cybernetics thousands of years ago. The power of suggestion has been proved to stop bleeding, make sick persons well, and to make weak people strong. In survival you may have to use this power to do the seemingly impossible, or to keep others with you from becoming non-effective workers.

The conscious level may determine you have a positive need. The subconscious recognizes this thought as a picture and relates that picture to other word pictures and habits previously gained, either positive or negative.

Suppose your subconscious recognizes the input as positive (good), so it passes it on to the creative reality level, along with the related "can do" thoughts needed to solve the problem. At the creative level your positive attitude allows you to try again and again to solve the problem. Each time you fail, you learn what won't work; but your "can do" attitude sees the goal and will solve the problem with time.

The true value of positive thinking rests in the ability to lock our negative thoughts and imaginations that distract from attaining the goal. The men who have researched this subject put it this way,

"The mind can heal the mind,
The mind can heal the body."

Prayer: Nearly every person who has survived a disaster or serious emergency admits to praying. Since one's prayers are personal, there is no need to attempt to explain, but only to accept the fact.

In effect, the victim is living each minute for itself -- forgetting the past, concentrating on the immediate problem and the consequences of his or her actions. The mind plays such a great part in any survival situation that a victim often allows future problems to overshadow the immediate needs of living.

Conservation of energy is controlled by the survivor's mind. Knowledge of energy use and loss will determine how long this limited supply will last. The mind, and the body with its limited amount of life-sustaining energy, make up the major factors that are prevalent in every survival situation. When either is uncontrolled, the other is sure to perish.

131

The importance of defensive action cannot be over-emphasized when endeavoring to stay alive under hostile conditions. Mountain rescue experts rely upon the following when advising what to do in any emergency:

S	Stop
T	Think
O	Observe
P	Plan

S -- Stop. The body is designed to do three things: digest food, do work, or think. It does not do any two of these very efficiently simultaneously. Hence the need to stop so that you can think. By stopping to think you may avoid the possible errors of hasty decisions.

T -- Think. Think about the immediate and future danger to self. Analyze the weather, the terrain and the available energy and resources to sustain life.

O -- Observe. Look around you, observing the problem for possible solutions. Observe resources, weather potential and best possible course of action.

P -- Plan. After thinking and observing all aspects of your emergency, plan a course of action which will best utilize your limited available energy. Plan your activities, whatever they may be, to take advantage of the natural and ready resources.

Some survival emergencies are recognized immediately, such as a downed airplane in the wilderness, or the sudden realization that you are completely lost or disoriented. Other survival situations develop slowly, often without being recognized until it is too late. It is these problems which possess the hidden dangers to life.

When reports of outdoor activity problems are analyzed, it becomes evident that often powerful motivations had a detrimental effect on judgment, mental attitude and the will to live. Evidence shows that these motivations may have even created the emergency situation.

Little is known about the psychological stress a human experiences when alone in unfamiliar surroundings. Stress which may cause a person to ignore the common sense rules of safety and good workmanship. The weekend adventurer, with a definite time limit or budget for his or her planned outing, feels compelled to wring the maximum enjoyment from each minute, delaying the return trip until the last possible moment. Although little can be done to prevent these stresses, it is important that they be noted here for your own evaluation.

The three factors noted here are carried into the outdoor environment by the recreationist and their combined effect can help to deteriorate judgment and precipitate accidents.

Determination: A state of mind which allows long-sought desires to overrule good judgment. An example of determination is the desire to reach a long sought, pre-set goal, whatever it may be, regardless of setbacks, storms, loss of equipment or danger to life. This attitude can push a person to use every ounce of energy to attain the goal, leaving none to sustain life during the return journey.

Determination "to do or die" may be a figure of speech, but all too often outdoor people will subject their bodies to near impossible tasks under the most severe weather conditions to reach a destination today, when tomorrow or next week the task would be a simple, pleasurable journey.

Promises: This single word quite possibly endangers more lives in our modern society than any other: "Honey, I promise I'll be home in time. " "Don't worry, Boss, I'll be to work on time. " "I'll be there at 6 p. m. sharp. " How often have you set yourself a seemingly possible time schedule, only to be delayed? Your promise now creates a stress situation which makes you hurry.

"Haste makes waste. "   "The hurrier I go the behinder I get. " These are sayings that have proven true in outdoor travel as well as on the highways. To keep promises people have been known to take dangerous shortcuts, run down slippery trails, push on in marginal weather, or travel in darkness. Even risk the lives of companions in an attempt to fulfill their promises.

Every person has responsibilities to himself or herself and to others, and each person assumes obligations which govern daily life. However, in outdoor travel away from civilization, a person's first and prime responsibility and obligation is to his or her body -- its warmth, its energy and its protection.

Get-home-itis: Another stress factor which can spur a person to disregard the sound precepts of safe outdoor travel. This pressure may be caused by obligations, promises, or even responsibilities that he or she feels must be honored at all costs. In an attempt to honor them good judgment is often forsaken in hopes he or she will be lucky and make it home to relieve these nagging pressures. In a sense home pressures overrule the common sense actions necessary to sustain and protect life while away from civilization and immediate help. Outdoor people should not under estimate the wrath of an irate loved one. But they must at times consider the worst of two evils: Being late and safely returning home, or pressing on in the face of a storm (instead of finding shelter) and never returning home.

The "challenge to stay alive" in hostile environments is a physical and a mental experience to a human. For humans to sustain life in any environment they must have air, body shelter, water and food, and the will to live. These are necessary for sustaining energy production and normal body functions.

How a person may acquire and utilize these necessities to maintain life is determined by the individual's brain. Thus the survivor's brain becomes his or her greatest asset, or most dangerous enemy in a survival situation where life is endangered. When a person is forced to adjust quickly from a civilized environment, with all its comforts, to an existence much like that of a cave dweller, psychological problems often develop. These are mental problems that can be detrimental to his or her situation of staying alive.

Doctors agree that basic fears do exist, and they acknowledge that under stress people are at the mercy of the mind. These may well be responsible for more deaths than exposure, hunger, or any other danger. FEAR and IMAGINATION plague almost every person who is face-to-face with possible death. Fearfulness that can turn to blind panic may cause an experienced, knowledgeable person to injure or even kill himself in the intensity of his terror.

Realizing that you will have fears and that these are normal emotions in unfamiliar situations, you will be aware of them and better able to cope with them as they appear. Fears can be expected in any survival situation in this order of importance:

Fear of being alone	Fear of suffering
Fear of animals	Fear of death
Fear of darkness	Fear of society

The fear of being alone can be a very serious emotion, when you think that you may never hear a human voice again. No radio, no companion, nothing but you, alone, against the thousands of unseen things lurking beyond the light of your survival fire. In the realm of unfamiliar environments a person is hopelessly at the mercy of the elements and terrain. Loneliness in such situations can become almost unbearable.

The fear of animals can be very real to a person in a strange, often foreboding environment. When all alone, let a twig snap in the darkness or a rustling occur in the brush nearby, and even the most experienced outdoor person will be startled and uneasy. You may know that animals are generally afraid of humans, but add a little imagination to these strange sounds and this nagging, minor fear can turn into terror.

The fear of darkness is inherent in most humans. Darkness immobilizes us, blinds us, and hides all familiar things, regardless of the environment. Darkness stirs the imagination and may let it run rampant.

The fear of suffering and death are normal emotions and understandable. No one likes to face suffering, even for a very short time. And the mind and imagination can distort a situation until it can truly become insufferable and perhaps contribute to death.

Fear of society -- reprisal, loss of face, ridicule -- or the fear of inconveniencing or worrying others.

Give-up-itis -- several other aspects of mental attitude must be considered detrimental to humans in survival situations. Give-up-itis is a mental reaction that leads to a do-nothing attitude, which could be the surest way to terminate your life. It represents a complete loss of the will to live, and has occurred even in short-term survival situations.

Panic -- the exact opposite of give-up-itis is panic, or the uncontrolled urge to hurry or run from the situation. Panic is triggered by the mind and imagination under stress. At the end of unchecked panic, when all available energy has been used, exhaustion and often death occur.

Knowing that fearfulness and imagination could be a great problem in any survival situation, you are forewarned and can take steps to limit their effect.

Energy Use and Loss of Energy -- At the outset of your survival situation you will have a limited amount of readily available energy. It may be large or small, depending upon the circumstances before the situation developed. If you were in a plane or vehicle, well fed, warm and rested, you would probably have a large supply of energy available. If you are hiking in hilly or rugged terrain and have been using your nuscle power most of the day, you may have nearly depleted your available energy supply.

The real challenge to stay alive is to use your brain to conserve this remaining amount of usable energy by limiting your muscle action and by reducing body heat loss. Your situation and actions must be carefully analyzed to determine the immediate and the most important needs to improve your chances of living and being rescued.

Often a person must expend energy to travel to a better location to eliminate energy loss due to weather exposure. Energy spent in improving shelter from wind, wetness and cold is energy well spent, because it improves your ability to conserve vital body heat. The challenge is to determine what energy to expend to gain the greatest return for the energy used.

ADEQUATE shelter is often the key to survival. Many people have preconceived ideas of what a wilderness shelter should be. But in a survival situation one must conserve one's limited energy with extreme care. Building an ideal, preconceived shelter may be too costly in energy, as well as insufficient to conserve body heat. Searching for sticks and boughs, lacing them into a shelter, may not be as practical as digging a small, body-sized cave under a downed log, with emphasis on insulation and dryness. The shelter <u>must provide</u> protection from convection and conduction of body heat. Your shelter is your home and the most vital part of your survival effort. It can make your survival a comfortable, tolerable wait for rescue or better traveling conditions.

<u>Resourcefulness</u> -- When survival is threatened and you have acknowledged the fact that you are scared, you must also acknowledge that you are not helpless. You have many items on your person that can be useful. You have to think like the 20th Century, educated person that you are, but place your thoughts in the cave dweller's level. After all, he and she lived in conditions far worse than your's and evolved to what you are today. Think basic needs when searching for the means for warmth, metal and wood for shelter from rain and wind.

If you are in an airplane, automobile, boat, or near any such object when a survival situation develops, stay near these valuable sources of material. Your resourcefulness at improvising your needs can mean the difference between life or death. The thinking person will survive because he or she recognizes the immediate and most important problem and has the confidence to mentally cope with it. Most important, he or she knows that there must be absolute control over all thoughts, imaginations and all physical movement.

TRIP EVALUATION

1. Do you feel the initial purpose of the trip was successfully achieved?

    Yes ( )   No ( )

    If no, please comment.

2. Please rate the following:

	Poor	Satisfactory	Good	Excellent
Dates for the trip	( )	( )	( )	( )
Pretrip evaluation system	( )	( )	( )	( )
Choice of group members	( )	( )	( )	( )
Area chosen for the trip	( )	( )	( )	( )
Pretrip planning	( )	( )	( )	( )
Seminars	( )	( )	( )	( )
Handouts	( )	( )	( )	( )
Food	( )	( )	( )	( )
Equipment Requirements	( )	( )	( )	( )
Transportation Arrange- ments	( )	( )	( )	( )
Hiking time per day	( )	( )	( )	( )
Hiking distance per day	( )	( )	( )	( )
Choice of campsites	( )	( )	( )	( )
Safety considerations	( )	( )	( )	( )
Pretrip leadership	( )	( )	( )	( )
Trip leadership	( )	( )	( )	( )
Cost of trip	( )	( )	( )	( )
Other_____	(( )	( )	( )	( )

3. How might future trips be improved?

4. If you had it to do all over again, would you have gone on the trip?

    Yes ( )   No ( )   Why?

5. Would you be interested in taking future trips with this or any other group?

    Yes ( )   No ( )   Why?

6. What did you most enjoy about the trip?

7. What did you least enjoy about the trip?

APPENDIX   U

TRIP BUDGET

Item	Estimated	Actual	Group Paid	Organization Paid	Other Paid
Transportation:					
Insurance					
Gas					
Oil					
Pretrip Servicing					
Safety equipment					
Tolls					
Maintenance (labor)					
Maintenance (parts)					
Road service/towing					
Parking					
Rental					
Public transportation					
Accommodations:					
Car campsite					
Backcountry campsites					
Entrance fee (User's fee)					
Motel/hotel					
Equipment:					
Purchases					
Rentals					
Food:					
On the road					
For the trail					
Repackaging supplies					

Trip Budget continued on page 139

138

TRIP BUDGET
(Continued)

Item	Estimated	Actual	Group Paid	Organization Paid	Other Paid
Miscellaneous:					
Leader's insurance					
Phone					
Postage					
Information packets					
Maps					
Guidebooks					
Transportation prior to trip					
Printing/ reproduction					
Books, pamphlets, brochures					
Services					
Other					
Total					

Amount estimated to be paid by group $_____

Amount estimated to be paid by organization $_____

Amount estimated to be paid by other $_____

Amount actually spent $_____

Amount refunded to group $_____

Amount refunded to organization $_____

Amount refunded to other $_____

Actual amount to be collected from group $_____

Actual amount to be collected from organization $_____

Actual amount to be collected from other $_____

139

APPENDIX V

LEGAL CONSIDERATIONS *

No climber would question the obligation to provide medical or evacuation assistance to another climber; none of the following comments should raise any doubts about this responsibility. However, for the sake of completeness, some discussion of the legal rights and obligations of persons rendering medical aid to others appears appropriate. These comments provide only a general outline of the laws applicable in the U.S. and Canada. Each state, province, and nation makes its own rules concerning many problems and the variation from place to place is often considerable.

Personal Liability

Almost no country has laws which require anyone to help a stranger in distress. A climber can decline to render first aid or assistance to a stranger found injured in the mountains with legal impunity. An obligation does exist in such circumstances, but the obligation is ethical, not legal.

A legal obligation to render first aid and assistance does exist when one has negligently caused injury to another. This obligation would probably exist when the injured person is a member of the same climbing party, even though the injury was caused by someone else or by chance.

Even though no one is required by law to render first aid, if assistance is undertaken, it must be performed in a reasonably careful manner. That is, one must exercise that care which an ordinarily prudent person would exercise under similar circumstances. Thus anyone rendering first aid is liable for harm to the injured person when harm could have been avoided by the exercise of reasonable care. A physician is held to a higher standard. He or she must conduct himself or herself as an ordinarily prudent doctor, not as a lay person. The need for knowledge of first aid by climbers is well recognized, and many of them have such knowledge. A climber could be held liable for injuries resulting from failure to be familiar with first aid techniques generally known to climbers if he or she had indicated in some manner beforehand that he or she did have such knowledge.

The circumstances in which assistance is rendered are also important. The care legally required is that which is reasonable under the circumstances. More severe disorders require closer attention and more extensive and sophisticated medical assistance. Yet the law also takes into account such factors as the location of the victim, any danger for the person rendering aid, the equipment available, and the physical condition of the parties.

Although a legal basis for claim does exist, lawsuits arising from voluntary medical assistance are very rare. In mountaineering circles they are essentially non-existent.

LEGAL ASPECTS OF ADVENTURE ACTIVITIES [1]

Betty van der Smissen

One of the most unfortunate circumstances which has arisen because of the ogre of liability is that any activity which appears to have some element of physical risk and mental courage is not permitted by many of our schools and municipalities in conducting both formal and extra-curricular programs. This has caused many of our programs to be "too soft, too dull, and too ordinary." It is therefore very pertinent to discuss the legal aspects of adventure activities so that those who are interested in such might have a better understanding of just what their liability might be.

In over 1,000 cases reviewed relating to liability and physical activity, no activity, except for boxing, has been considered inherently hazardously dangerous. This is not to say that some activities do not involve more risk and thus require more of the participant both physically and mentally, and of the teacher or leader, therefore, more care; but, it does say that the risks which give rise to law suits are based in negligence, negligence of people, not the hazards of an activity -- hazardous people, rather than hazardous activities. This might be referred to as "people risks," rather than "activity risks."

Negligence occurs when one owes a duty to protect the participant from unreasonable risks which might foreseeably harm him or her and such duty is not performed adequately. Thus, those who say that there is more likelihood of liability suits and a greater risk involved in conducting adventure activities approach the situation in an incorrect manner. As far as the basic principles of negligence are concerned, there is no difference between an adventure activity and any other activity being conducted. The very same principles for safely conducting such activities apply to all types of activities.

Basic General Principle

The fundamental questions are -- How do I minimize law suits? How do I protect against such suits being filed? If one is filed, what can I do? Law suits seem to be a way of life and there is really no point in being scared that one might be sued -- we just have to do the best we can. One cannot protect 100 percent -- let's face it. We need to be realistic about law suits -- and about safety practices. In the following sections are some guidelines which will help minimize suits being filed, and if they are filed, will serve you well, if they are followed, as a defense.

The overriding question involved in all of these guidelines is -- With what standard of care must one perform? The standard of care which must be performed can be answered by a general principle -- One must be a "reasonable and prudent professional." Often one hears that it is required that one be a "reasonable and prudent person"; but, that is not enough. One is required to be a professional. You must have the competence required for the role you have accepted. If you hold yourself out to be qualified to instruct or lead rock climbing, then you are saying that you know the proper procedures for rock climbing. It is irrelevant whether or not you actually do know the proper techniques and procedures . . . the court will hold that you must perform as if you do if you are undertaking such role of leadership. It therefore behooves you to be well versed and qualified in whatever adventure activity you are engaging.

One might also ask -- What is professional conduct? It is knowing the "best practices" of the profession and being up-to-date on the latest developments as to technique and procedure. Professional conduct in terms of guidelines is considered in three aspects: (1) Supervision; (2) Conduct of activity; and (3) Safety Equipment and Procedures.

Supervision

Supervision is one of the critical elements giving rise to law suits, and this is of particular importance in the adventure activities. There are three aspects concerning supervision which should be given particular attention.

Direct v. General Supervision. Situations should be distinguished which require general supervision, specific supervision, or no supervision, for the nature of the required action by the leader is dependent thereon. By general supervision is meant that an individual must be within the activity area overseeing the activity, while specific supervision means being at the specific location of activity with the participants. The location of the supervisor is of importance in general supervision. The supervisor (leader or instructor) must be immediately accessible to anyone who needs him or her. The supervisor must never leave the area, for to do so opens wide the door for law suits. If injury occurs, a competent person should be secured to either take the injured to medical attention or to give supervision to the group. Also in terms of location, the supervisor must be able to oversee the entire program systematically, that is, rotate to all parts of the activity area. Another consideration for general supervision is that the supervisor must be alert to conditions which may be dangerous to participants in the general area in which the activity is taking place, which includes lack of protective devices or safety equipment as well as the participants going beyond their capabilities. Not only should a professional be able to identify such dangerous conditions, but he or she must also be able to anticipate and teach toward safe practices. The activity is not dangerous in and of itself, but becomes so because of the situation or conditions within which it is conducted.

A second consideration of supervision is that of specific supervision, which must be given when introducing an activity to a participant or participant group until each person is familiar enough with the activity so that each appreciates the activity in terms of the person's capacity to do the activity, as well as understand and adhere to the safety practices and procedures established by the leader. The appreciation of the activity and understanding of the safety procedures are essential if the defense of assumption of risk is to be used in case of suit. It has often been said, especially in sports, that the participant assumes the risks -- but cases in the last few years have put a new emphasis on the responsibility of the leader -- <u>a participant does not assume any risks of which he is not aware and appreciates!!</u> This places the burden on the leader for appropriately communicating the risks involved and ascertaining whether the participant thoroughly understands. Some have referred to this informing and subsequent participation as "advise and consent." There is much more to this advising and consenting than appears on the surface. It is important that it be noted that knowledge of a risk is insufficient, that is, it is not sufficient merely to inform or warn of risks in an activity; there must be an understanding and appreciation of that risk. This appreciation of risk works both ways, that is, the inexperience of a participant requires greater effort on the part of the leader to communicate the risks; and, on the other hand, if a performer is young but inexperienced, he is held to assume those risks of which he is knowledgeable through experience and thus would be deemed to have an appreciation thereof. Appreciation extends to both experienced and inexperienced, and also to those of mental capability and incapability. This concept of appreciation of risk is extremely important in the adventure activities and it behooves every leader to become a communicator par excellent!!

It should be pointed out that during an activity going on under general supervision if any change in the condition of the participant is noted, such as over fatigue or apparent lack of appreciation of dangers, or there is failure to adhere to rules and regulations, the leader must change from general to specific supervision until the situation is back to "normal." In the identification of such change of condition of participant, a high level of professional ability is required to observe this change while activity is underway. Once spotting change in a participant's condition that person's activity must be modified accordingly.

A third aspect of supervision is that which relates to knowledge of first aid and emergency care. Such knowledge is absolutely essential. A considerable number of cases have turned on improper first aid practices. Holding a Red Cross First Aid Certificate, regardless of what level of expertise, does not in any way protect. It is only evidence to the hiring administrator or supervisor that such person has satisfactorily completed such course. The critical element in any law suit is what was done. A person must not only know what to do, but must be able to react promptly. The first aid and emergency care must cover not only those aspects in a "regular" first aid course, but must include emergency care pertinent to the type of situation in which the leader is involved. Again, this means that the emergency care particular to a special adventure activity, such as mountain climbing injuries, must be learned. Every director of an adventure activity should see to it that his or her staff has not only a first aid refresher course but also an up-to-date briefing on the most desirable first aid practices. The emergency procedures, too, should be well established and the staff very familiar with them.

Conduct of Activity

As previously mentioned, seldom is an activity considered inherently hazardously dangerous, but it is the manner of conducting the activity which is critical. There are several aspects of this which must be given particular attention for the adventure activities. First is the adequacy and progression of instruction. It is extremely important that not only the leader be very competent in instructing in these particular activities, but also that the progression of such activity instruction be proper. One should know well the sequence of difficulty of various skills, and the experiences in which a participant engages should be sequenced according to the development of skill competency. If one is going to introduce adventure activities into the program, it behooves such director to be sure that competent instructional staff is obtained.

A second consideration in the conduct of the activity, so very important in adventure activity where physical endurance and mental courage are integral, is that of the maturity and condition of the participant. Not only must the leader be able to teach a skill, as indicated in the foregoing paragraph, but also must understand the human being biologically and psychologically and the relationship of the physical activity thereto. At all times the instructor or leader must be alert to the physical condition and psychological state of the participant. The instructor must also sufficiently know the capacities and capabilities of the participants so that appropriate groupings and activities may be used in relation to such capacities and capabilities.

As indicated in the foregoing section on Supervision, the direct or specific supervision must be given when instructing initially an adventure activity. In such instruction it is important that the participant learns to appreciate the risks involved and the procedures for safety. The instructor must be alert to possible danger points in performance and appropriate caution and necessity for greater competence in performance of the particular skill emphasized.

Safety Equipment and Environmental Condition

In many of the adventure activities the most important aspect of safety is in the equipment. For example, one would not think of going rock climbing with defective ropes! It is the responsibility of the leadership to provide a safe environment, although one is not an insurer of safety. Not only should the equipment be appropriate to the participant's size and experience, but it also must be of good quality so that it will adequately protect the user. All equipment should be carefully inspected prior to each use and repaired immediately when needed, or replaced if it is no longer safe. Considerable care must be given to correcting any dangerous condition regarding equipment.

The environmental conditions also must be given attention as far as safety is concerned. If there is high wind or thunderstorms which interfere with the safety of the performance of the activity, then the activity must be appropriately modified so as not to give undue risk to the participants. To assess environmental conditions in terms of safety takes a person experienced in the activity.

In regard to both equipment and environmental conditions, safety rules, regulations and procedures must be established and adhered to. There must be no permissiveness allowed participants when it comes to a matter of safety..

In summary, it should again be emphasized as pointed out initially that one must not leave out adventure activities just because of fear of liability suits. What is crucial is the standard of care exercised to protect the participant from undue risk of harm. Knowledge of the activity in terms of appropriate techniques and equipment for varying levels of experience and environmental conditions is essential . . . and are not these the same requirements as for any activity? If the leadership is well prepared, conduct your adventure activities with confidence!

[1] Based on presentation at Lorado Taft Field Campus, Northern Illinois University, April 20, 1975. For further details regarding the substance of the presentation, see the book: Van der Smissen, Legal Liability of Cities and Schools, Cincinnati: W. H. Anderson, Legal Publishers, 1968, Supplement, 1975.

Betty van der Smissen is Professor of Recreation and Member of the Bar, The Pennsylvania State University.

APPENDIX W

BIBLIOGRAPHY *

The following is a bibliographical listing of supplementary reading. The listing is categorized to help the reader find pertinent material more easily. The categories correspond to the chapters of the thesis in the following manner:

PURPOSE:
    Chapter 1 -- "PURPOSE FOR A GROUP BACKPACKING TRIP"

PLANNING:
    Chapter 2 -- "SELECTING GROUP MEMBERS"
    Chapter 3 -- "SELECTING TRIP DATES"
    Chapter 4 -- "SELECTING A TRIP LOCATION"
    Chapter 5 -- "TRANSPORTATION"
    Chapter 8 -- "GROUP MEETINGS"
    Chapter 9 -- "POST TRIP ACTIVITIES"
    Chapter 12 -- "BUDGET"

FOOD & COOKING:
    Chapter 6 -- "FOOD & COOKING"

EQUIPMENT
    Chapter 7 -- "EQUIPMENT"

CAMP & TRAIL ACTIVITIES:
    Chapter 9 -- "TRAIL ACTIVITIES & TECHNIQUES"
    Chapter 10 -- "CAMP ACTIVITIES & TECHNIQUES"

SAFETY:
    Covers all chapters

GENERAL:
    Covers all chapters. These books usually incorporate all aspects of backpacking.

* NOTE: Those books and articles the author believes to be of superior quality have been marked with an asterisk. (*).

Cardwell, P. Camping tips: QED: PR PDQ. Wilderness Camping, 1973, 3(2), 54-55.

Danielson, J.A. How to get started winter backpacking. Backpacker, 1976, 4(1), 54-57.

Dannen, K. Nature study vacation. Backpacker, 1975, 3(4), 41-42.

Doan, M. S. Turning children into backpackers. Backpacker, 1977, 5(2), 22-27; 71-72.

*Drasdo, H. Education and the mountain centres (2nd ed.). Melin-Y-Coed, Llanwst, Denbighshire, England: Tyddyn Gabriel, 1973.

Frisch, B. Silence and magic. Backpacker, 1973, 1(4), 30-31; 90.

Hahn, V., & Hahn, B. More than a challenge. Wilderness Camping, 1973, 3(4), 46-48.

Hindert, D. Guide to ski-backpacking. Backpacking Journal, Fall-Winter 1975, pp. 72-73; 92.

*Hope, J. Outing impact. Backpacker, 1973, 1(1), 28-31; 81.

*Howe, H., Unsoeld, W., & Kelly, F. J. Major papers presented at the conference on experiential education. Unpublished manuscript, 1974. (Available from (Maria Snyder, Colorado Outward Bound School, Box 9038, South Denver Station, Denver, Colorado)).

Kals, W. S. How to tell the stars. Backpacker, 1976, 5(5), 45-49; 73-76.

Kelly, J.F., & Baer, D. J. Outward Bound schools as an alternative to institutionalization for adolescent delinquent boys. Unpublished manuscript, 1968. (Available from (Colorado Outward Bound School, P.O. Box 7247, Denver, Colorado 80207)).

Kemsley, Jr., W. Can backpacking be a mystical trip? Backpacker, 1974, 2(2), 38-43.

Kemsley, Jr., W. Editorial: Limits on groups. Backpacker, 1975, 3(2), 4.

*Kesselheim, D. A. A rationale for outdoor activity as experimental education: A reason for freezin'. Unpublished manuscript, 1974. (Available from (School of Education, University of Massachusetts, Amherst, Massachusetts)).

*Lowry, T. (Ed.). Camping Therapy: Its uses in psychiatry and rehabilitation. Springfield, Illinois: Charles C. Thomas, 1974.

148

*Manning, H. Where did all these damn hikers come from? Backpacker,
    1975, 3(2), 36-41; 83-85.

Mason, B. V. College outdoor programs: An alternative to traditional
    outdoor recreation. Unpublished, manuscript, n.d. (Available
    from (Outdoor Program, ERB Memorial Union, University of Oregon,
    Eugene, Oregon)).

*Metcalfe, J. A. Adventure programming. University Park, New Mexico:
    New Mexico State University, 1976. (ERIC Document Reproduction
    Service No. ED 118 336).

Nero, B. The deeper the stream, The longer it sounds. Backpacker, 1973,
    1(2), 60-63; 98.

Nold, J. J. Outward Bound approaches to alternative schooling. Unpub-
    lished manuscript, 1973. (Available from (Colorado Outward Bound
    School, P.O. Box 7247, Denver, Colorado 80207)).

Perry, P.M. Backpacking-101. Backpacker, 1974, 2(1), 68-76.

*Petzolt, P. Adventure education and the national outdoor leadership
    school. Journal of Outdoor Education, 1975, 10(1), 3-7.

*Project Adventure. Teaching through adventure: A practical approach.
    Hamilton, Massachusetts: Author, 1976.

Schabel, A. E. What do you mean up, We never came down. Backpacker,
    1976, 4(4), 42-44; 70.

Stark, M. Any woman can. Wilderness Camping, 1975, 5(4), 24-25.

Vandervelde, M. Boys with outdoor interest seldom go wrong. Wilderness
    Camping, 1972, 2(5), 18-19.

PLANNING

Asa, W. How far? How fast? Wilderness Camping, 1975, 5(4), 26-27.

Aune, M. J. Efficient pack loading. Wilderness Camping, 1977, 7(2),
    24-25.

Braasch, G. A. Orientation to map making. Backpacker, 1973, 1(3),
    32-35; 98-102.

*Crain, J., & Milne, T. Camping without gasoline. Westminster, Mary-
    land: Random, 1974.

Cunningham, G. How to keep warm. Denver: An Outdoor Sports Company,
    1972.

*Disley, J. Your way with map and compass. Willowdale, Ontario: Canadian Orienteering Service, 1971.

Disley, J. Orienteering. Harrisburg, Pennsylvania: Stackpole, 1973.

Eagerbretson, D. L. Physical conditioning for the wilderness camper. Wilderness Camping, 1971, 1(3), 13-15.

*Fear, E. Where am I: A text and workbook for personal navigation. Tacoma, Washington: Survival Education Association, 1974.

*Fitzwilliams, J. (Ed.) Guidelines for individual behavior and citizen input for trail related activities. Washington, D.C.: Appalachian Trail Club, 1974.

Garvey, E. Appalachian hiker. Oakton, Virginia: Appalachian Books. 1971.

*Goddard, E. H. A trail profile: Why? How? Cupertino, California: Antelope Camping Equipment, 1975.

Greenhood, D. Mapping. Chicago: University of Chicago Press, 1971.

Hardin, D., & Kelly, B. You and your gear--Physical fitness. Backpacker, 1975, 3(4), 28-31.

Hayes, C. Recipe for statistics. Wilderness Camping, 1973, 3(1), 16-18.

Henderson, J. Run your way to wilderness fitness. Wilderness Camping, 1975, 5(4), 41-44.

*How to keep your feet warm. Backpacker, 1977, 5(1), 50-57.

Kjellstrom, B. Be expert with map and compass. Harrisburg, Pennsylvania: Stackpole, 1972.

Lobeck, A. Things maps don't tell us. Riverside, New Jersey: Macmillan, 1956.

McKay, R. D. Planning and developing a model curriculum in outdoor re- creation management with particular emphasis for United States International University. (Doctoral dissertation, United States International University, 1975.) Dissertation Abstracts Interna- tional (University Microfilms No. 75-29, 397).

McLeod, R. A planning guide for short backpacking and ski touring courses with Colorado Outward Bound School. Unpublished manus- cript, 1976. (Available from Colorado Outward Bound School, Box 9038, South Denver Station, Denver, Colorado).

*Meyer-Ardent, J.R.   Mountain weather. Off Belay, April 1977,
     pp. 13-17.

Mitchell, J., & Fear, E. Fundamentals of outdoor enjoyment. Tacoma,
     Washington: Survival Education Association, 1977.

*Mooers, R. Finding your way out-of-doors. New York, 1972.

Nordstrom, F. Shaping up. Backpacker, 1974, 2(1), 61+.

*Nutter, J., Cohen, M., & Cohen, S. A mountain classroom: A guide for
     teachers and youth leaders. Boston: Appalachian Mountain Clubs,
     1975.

Prater, G. Snowshoeing. Tacoma, Washington: Mountaineers, 1974.

Project Adventure. Project Adventure. Hamilton, Massachusetts: Author,
     1974.

Roscoe, D. T. Mountaineering: A manual for teachers and instructors.
     London: Faber and Faber, 1976.

Rutstrum, C. The wilderness route finder. Riverside, New Jersey:
     Collier, 1967.

*Simpson, B. Initiative games. Butler, Pennsylvania: Author, 1974.

Silverman, G. Backpacking with babies and small children. Lynwood,
     Washington: Signpost Publications, 1974.

Steinberg, J.M. Bus stop trails of the northwest. Hiking, Summer
     1974, pp. 62-69.

Stout, J., & Stout, A. Backpacking with small children. New York:
     Funk & Wagnalls, 1975.

Sussman, A, & Goods, R. The magic of walking. New York: Simon &
     Schuster, 1967.

Tacoma Mountain Rescue. Maps: Street signs of the wilderness.
     Tacoma, Washington: Author, n.d.

*Van der Smissen, Betty. Legal aspects of adventure activities.
     Journal of Outdoor Education, 1975, 10(1), 12-15.

*Van Matre, S. Acclimatization. Martinsville, Indiana: American
     Camping Association, 1972.

Vinal, W. G. Nature recreation (2nd ed.) New York, Dover, 1963.

Wildoner, D. Backpacking in desert country. <u>Wilderness Camping</u>, 1972, <u>2</u>(1), 24-28.

Wright, R. H. The mosquito: Know thine enemy. <u>Backpacker</u>, 1977, <u>5</u>(3), 62-65.

FOOD AND COOKING

Adlhoch, R. Paraphernalia: Cooking in your sleeping bag. <u>Off Belay</u>, January 1977, pp. 31; 33.

Backcountry breakfasts. <u>Backpacker</u>, 1976, <u>4</u>(2), 64-68.

Baker, H. The one burner gourmet: Great Lakes Press, 1975.

Bergh, M. The basic wok-er: Oriental trail foods are here, <u>Hiking</u>, Summer 1974, pp. 58-61.

*Best of freeze-dried dinners. <u>Backpacker</u>, 1974, <u>2</u>(3), 63-80.

Bradley, M. At last, A lightweight oven. <u>Hiking</u>, Summer 1974, pp. 70-72.

Bunnelle, H. <u>Food for knapsackers: And other trail travelers.</u> Totowa, New Jersey: Sierra Press, 1971.

Bunnelle, H., & Saruis, S. <u>Cooking for camp and trail,</u> Totowa, New Jersey: Sierra Press, 1972.

*Carper, J. <u>The brand name nutrition counter.</u> New York: Bantam, 1975.

*Cook, M., & Fiske, J. <u>Backpackers' cook book.</u> Berkeley, California: Ten Speed Press, 1973.

Crocker, D. W. Fireless foods. <u>Wilderness Camping,</u> 1976, <u>6</u>(2), 25-28.

*Drew, E. P. <u>The complete light-pack camping and trail-foods cookbook.</u> New York: McGraw-Hill, 1977.

Engers, M. Going light with saijo. <u>Backpacker</u>, 1975, <u>3</u>(4), 39.

Ewald, E. B. How to go vegetarian. <u>Backpacker</u>, 1975, <u>3</u>(4), 31-33.

Ford, D. Kephart on survival rations. <u>Wilderness Camping</u>, 1974, <u>4</u>(4), 30-32.

Ford, F. Pack to nature: <u>Nutrition made easy in the house or in the woods.</u> n.p., 1974.

*Forgey, W. <u>The complete guide to trail food use.</u> Pittsboro, Indiana: Indiana Camp Supply, 1976.

Garret, F. The backpacker's guide to edible wild plants. Backpacker, 1974, 2(4), 30-31.

Griffin, T. Backpack trail cooking. New York: Sentinel, n.d.

Hall, A. The wild food trail guide. New York: Rinehart & Winston, 1976.

How to round out your freeze-dried dinner menu. Backpacker, 1975, 3(2), 64-72.

Jacobson, C. A pan for all seasons. Backpacker, 1977, 5(3), 25-27.

Jacobson, C. L. Wilderness meal. St. Paul, Minnesota: Minnesota Department of Natural Resources, Bureau of Information and Education, n.d.

Kinmont, V. Simple foods for the pack. Totowa, New Jersey: Sierra Press, 1976.

*MacManimann. Dry it, You'll like it. Seattle, Washington: Montana Books, 1974.

McMillan, D. The portable feast. Totowa, New Jersey: One Hundred Books, 1969.

Miller, D. The healthy trail food book. n.p., 1976.

*Pallister, N. Nolls cookery. Emporia, Kansas: Teachers College Press, 1974.

Saijo, A. Go-light backpacking. Backpacker, 1973, 1(3), 86-90.

Sign Post Publications. Pack rat papers # 2. Lynwood, Washington: Author, 1973.

Thoman, D. Roughing it easy. Provo, Utah: Brigham Young Press, 1974.

Wagner, R. Gorp. Off Belay, June 1974, p. 17.

Walley, J. Z. A garden in your pack. Wilderness Camping, 1976, 6(1), 24-25.

Wood, R. S. Pleasure packing--Tips on better eating. Wilderness Camping, 1973, 3(4), 49-51.

Van Lear, D. You and your gear -- Supermarket substitutes. Backpacker, 1974, 2(2), 26-29.

EQUIPMENT

Angier, B. Wilderness gear you can make. Riverside, New Jersey:
    Collier, 1973.

*Backpacking Clothing 1. Backpacker, 1975, 3(3), 51-59.

*Backpacking stoves, Part 1. Backpacker, 1976, 4(3), 65-69.

*Backpacking stoves, Part II. Backpacker, 1976, 4(4), 46-57.

Bentley, J. You and your gear--Care and repair of tents. Backpacker,
    1973, 1(3), 16-17.

Blackmer, D. Foam sleeping bags. Wilderness Camping, 1971, 1(3), 8-12.

Consumer Guide (Ed.). Camping and backpacking equipment test reports.
    New York: New American Library, 1974.

Cunningham, G., & Hasson, M. Lightweight camping equipment and how to
    make it. Totowa, New Jersey: Scribner's, 1976.

Curtis, S. The tarp: Don't leave home without it. Backpacking Journal,
    Summer 1977, pp. 26-27; 90.

*Do-it-yourself kits. Backpacker, 1976, 5(5), 50-57.

Dodd, H. The cutting edge. Wilderness Camping, 1977, 6(5). 14-16.

Engerbretson, D. Sewing to reap savings. Backpacking Journal, Fall-
    Winter 1975, pp. 74-75.

*Ford, D. New products review--Oh, Sears and Roebuck. Wilderness
    Camping, 1973, 3(1), 42-44.

Futterman, S. Soft house. New York: Harper & Row, 1976.

Green, F. The U.S. Army's tropical boot takes to the trail. Wilderness
    Camping, 1972, 2(5), 15-17.

*How to buy a compass. Backpacker, 1976, 4(1), 64-73.

*How to buy multi-person tents. Backpacker, 1977, 5(2), 53-68.

*How to buy snowshoes. Backpacker, 1973, 3(4), 62-66.

*How to stack up--Snowshoes. Backpacker, 1973, 3(4), 67-71.

*How to build a trail bed. Backpacker, 5(3), 66-76.

*Kemsley, W. (Ed.). Backpacking equipment. Riverside, New Jersey:
    Macmillan, 1975.

154

Kutik, W. You and your gear—Aboard a plane. Backpacker, 1973. 1(1), 12-13.

Masia, S. You and your gear—Breaking in boots. Backpacker, 1973, 1(4), 16-17.

Osgood, W., & Horley, C. The snowshoe book. Brattleboro, Vermont: Seth Green Press, 1971.

Perrin, A. (Ed.). Explorers Limited Source book. New York: Harper & Row, 1973.

Potomac Appalachian Trail Club. Lightweight equipment for hiking, camping and mountaineering. Washington, D.C.: Author, 1972.

*Richards, D. B. Compasses for wilderness travelers. Wilderness Camping, 1972, 2(1), 19-21.

Rubens, P. Bag tests: Down. Hiking, Summer 1974, pp. 44-53.

Self, C. Footwear. Backpacking Journal, Spring, 1977, pp. 30-32.

Wodraska, B. Survival staff. Wilderness Camping, 1972, 2(4), 26-27.

Wood, R. S. Boots for backpackers. Wilderness Camping, 1972, 2(2), 21-23.

Wood, R. S. Pleasure packing—The wrap-around frame. Wilderness Camping, 1972, 2(4), 14-15.

Wood, R. S. Pleasure packing—Outdoor insulation: Down vs. dacron vs. foam, part 1. Wilderness Camping, 1973, 3(1), 8-11.

Wood, R. S. Pleasure packing—Outdoor insulation: down vs. dacron vs. foam, part 2. Wilderness Camping, 1973, 3(2), 16-19.

Wood, R. S. Pleasure packing—Buying boots. Wilderness Camping, 1973, 3(3), 12; 14-15.

Wyman, D. Opinion: Sneakers are a shoe-in. Backpacking Journal, Fall-Winter 1975, p. 6.

CAMP AND TRAIL TECHNIQUES

Anderson, D. How to build a campfire in deep snow. Backpacker, 1974, 2(4), 33.

*Boudreau, T. M. Opinion: Slowing down. Backpacking Journal, Spring 1977, pp. 6-8.

Cunningham, G. How to camp and leave no trace. Denver: Gerry: An Outdoor Sports Company, 1972.

Curtis, S. Opinion: Backcountry ethic. Backpacking Journal, Summer 1977, pp. 13-15.

*Denney, R. M. A primer for field sanitation. Hiking, Summer 1974, pp. 88-89.

Henley, T. How to build an igloo. Backpacker, 1974, 2(4), 54-57.

*Pace, F. Yoga breath training. Off Belay, January 1977, pp 14-16.

Placek, B. Boy Scouts . . . Bury the hatchet. Backpacker, 1973, 1(1), 64-66.

*Ross, R. N. The mechanics of walking. Wilderness Camping, 1973, 3(3), 28-30.

Rubens, P., & Spaier, B. Fresh water--Fast. Hiking, Summer 1974, pp. 22-23.

Sand, G. Y. Opinion: Stop picking the plants. Backpacking Journal, Summer 1977, pp. 18-21.

Sumner, D. Snow caves: A lesson from the ptarmigan. Backpacker, 1977, 5(1), 29-31; 63-66.

*Walbridge, C. How to handle a heavy pack. Wilderness Camping, 1975, 5(3), 26-28.

*Waterman, G., & Waterman, L. How to keep warm in winter without a campfire. Backpacker, 1974, 2(4), 32.

Wood, R. S. Wilderness clean-up. Wilderness Camping, 1972, 2(3), 16-17.

SAFETY

*Adirondack Mountain Club. The bear facts. Glen Falls, New York: Author, 1975.

Adirondack Mountain Club. Hypothermia. Glens Falls, New York: Author, 1975.

Allen, D. Don't die on the mountain. Boston: Appalachian Mountain Club, 1972.

Appalachian Mountain Club. Mountain medicine symposium. Boston: Author, 1970.

*Arnold, R. What to do about bites and stings of venomous animals. Riverside, New Jersey: Collier, 1973.

Bangs, C. Sudden survival. <u>Off Belay</u>, December 1974, pp. 10-17.

Berglund, B. <u>Wilderness survival</u>. Totowa, New Jersey: Scribner's, 1972.

Brandner, G. <u>Living off the land</u>. New York: Galahad Books, 1974.

Burns: Cold water treatment. <u>Off Belay</u>, October 1974, pp. 13-14.

*Cheney, A. E. How dry I am: Thirst, dehydration, and water management. <u>Off Belay</u>, April 1977, pp. 23-25.

*Childs, Geoffrey. Lightning almost always strikes twice. <u>Backpacker</u>, 1973, <u>1</u>(2), 28-31.

Curtis, S. High there. <u>Backpacking Journal</u>, Spring 1977, pp. 33-36.

Dalrymple, B. <u>Survival in the outdoors</u>. New York: Dutton, 1972.

*Darvil, F. <u>Mountaineering medicine</u>. Mt. Vernon, Washington: Darvil Outdoors, 1975.

Dayton, L.B., & Arnold, J.W. Hydraulic sarong: Emergency treatment for hypothermic casualties. Off Belay, June 1975, pp. 2; 4.

*Eastman, P. Thermal injuries. <u>Backpacker</u>, 1977, <u>5</u>(3), 57-60; 95-98.

*Engerbretson, D. Too hot to trot. <u>Backpacking Journal</u>, Summer 1977, pp. 22-23; 78.

*Fear, E. Outdoor Living: Problems, solutions, guidelines. Tacoma, Washington: Survival Education Association, 1971.

*Fear, E. <u>Surviving the unexpected: A curriculum guide for wilderness survival and survival from natural and man made disasters</u>. Tacoma, Washington: Survival Education Association, 1974.

*Fear, E. <u>Surviving the unexpected wilderness emergency</u>. Tacoma, Washington: Survival Education Association, 1974.

Feldman, K., & Herndon, P. High altitude pulmonary edema. <u>Off Belay</u>, June 1977, pp. 2-5.

Francis, B. Head injuries. <u>Off Belay</u>, August 1975, pp. 17-19.

Fraser. <u>Avalanche enigma</u>. New York: Rand McNally, 1966.

*Gallagher, D. (Ed.). <u>Snowy torrents</u>. Alta, Utah: Alta Avalanche Study Center, 1967.

Gaston, M. I. Bug off: The anguished outdoorsman's guide to insect repellents. <u>Hiking</u>, Summer 1974, pp. 54-57.

Graves, R. Bushcraft: A serious guide to survival and camping. New York: Schocken, 1972.

Heiller, D. Stranded! Backpacker, 1976, 4(2), 37-40; 70-77.

Johann, E. Lost? You're not lost, You're right here. Seattle, Washington: Northwest Mountaineering Guide Service, 1971.

*Kahn, F. H., & Visscher, B. R. Is it safe? Off Belay, June 1977, pp. 23-24.

Kinnerr, G. R., & Cundiff, D. E. Padded hip belts: Their effect on exercise heart rate. Off Belay, August 1974, pp. 6-8.

*La Chapelle. A.B.C.s of avalanche safety. Denver: Highlander Publications, 1961.

*Lathrop, T. Hypothermia: Killer of the unprepared. Portland, Oregon: Mazamas, 1972.

Linsky, M. Death on a mountain. Backpacker, 1976, 4(1), 51-53; 80.

Martin, E. Hypothermia: A killer for all seasons. Wilderness Camping, 1973, 3(1), 38-41.

Mellor, M. Searching for avalanche victims. Off Belay, December 1975, pp. 10-15.

Merrill, B. The survival handbook. New York: Arc Books, 1974.

Meyers, G. Heat stress. Wilderness Camping, 1976, 6(2), 37-39.

*Meyer-Arendt, J. Frostbite--Signs, prevention, and treatment. Off Belay, December 1974, pp. 2-6.

Meyer-Arendt, J. What's new about avalanches? Off Belay, December 1974, pp. 7-9.

*Mitchell, D. Mountaineering first aid. Seattle, Washington: The Mountaineers, 1972.

Mitchell, D. What would you do? Part 2: Responding to an accident situation. Off Belay, April 1974, pp. 9-11.

Moran, M. Avalanche. Mariah, Winter 1976, pp. 26-33; 60.

Nelson, D., & Nelson, S. Desert survival. Tombstone, Arizona: Tecolote Press, 1975.

*Neuwirth, J. G. Principles of cold weather adaptability. Wilderness Camping, 1973, 3(6), 26-31.

Nordic World. All about winter safety. Mountain View, California: World Publications, 1975.

Nourse, A. E. Cold-weather killers: Hypothermia and frostbite. Backpacker, 1973, 1(4). 36-39; 81-85.

Nourse, A. The outdoorsman's medical guide. New York: Harper & Row, 1974.

Olsen, L. D. Outdoor survival skills. Provo, Utah: Brigham Young University Press, 1973.

Olsen, L. D. Wilderness survival. North Brunswick, New Jersey: Boy Scouts of America, 1974.

*Paulcke, W., & Dumler, H. Hazards in mountaineering. E. N. Bowman, trans. New York: Oxford University Press, 1973. (Originally published, 1933.

Platt, C. Outdoor survival. New York: Watts, 1976.

*Ross, R. A. Blisters. Wilderness Camping, 1975, 5(3), 29-31.

*Sandell, R. Out in the midday sun: Dehydration and the human body. Off Belay, June 1974, pp. 8-14.

Shockley, R. Survival in the wilds. South Brunswick, New Jersey, Barnes, 1970.

Smith, V. Western poison oak--Rhus Diversiloba. Off Belay, January 1977, p. 43.

*Steinberg, J.M. Avalanche: How to avoid them and what to do if . . . Backpacker, 1973, 3(4), 44-48; 83-87.

Tacoma Mountain Rescue. Fatigue and exhaustion. Tacoma, Washington: Author, n.d.

Tacoma Mountain Rescue. Hiking and backpacking safety. Tacoma, Washington: Author, n.d.

Tacoma Mountain Rescue. Hypothermia. Tacoma, Washington: Author, n.d.

Tacoma Mountain Rescue. Survival. Tacoma, Washington: Author, n.d.

*Washborn, B. Frost-bite: What it is, How to prevent it, and emergency treatment. Boston: Museum of Science, 1963.

*Wilkerson, J. (Ed.). Medicine for mountaineering. Seattle, Washington: Mountaineers, 1976.

GENERAL

Abel, M. Backpacking made easy. Healdsburg, California: Naturegraph, 1975.

Adirondack Mountain Club. For the beginning hiker. Glens Falls, New York: Author, n.d.

Adirondack Mountain Club. For the summer backpacker. Glens Falls, New York: Author, 1975.

Adirondack Mountain Club. For the winter mountaineer. Glens Falls, New York: Author, 1975.

Angier,B. Home in your pack. Riverside, New Jersey: Collier, 1972.

Booth, D. The backpackers handbook. London: Hale, 1972.

Boy Scouts of America. Fieldbook. North Brunswick, New Jersey: Author, 1967.

Bridge, R. America's backpacking book. Totowa, New Jersey: Scribner's, 1976.

Bridge, R. The complete snow camper's guide. Totowa, New Jersey: Scribner's, 1973.

Brower, D. (Ed.). The Sierra Club wilderness handbook. Westminster, Maryland: Ballantine, 1971.

Camp Trails. How to travel light. Phoenix, Arizona: Author, n.d.

Cheney, T. Camping by backpack and canoe. New York: Funk and Wagnalls, 1970.

Colby, C., & Angier, B. The art and science of taking to the woods. Riverside, New Jersey: Macmillan, 1971.

Colwell, R. Introduction to backpacking. Harrisburg, Pennsylvania: Stackpole, 1970.

*Danielson, J. Winter camping and hiking. Glen Falls, New York: Adirondack Mountain Club, 1972.

Elman, R. Hiker's bible. Garden City, New Jersey: Doubleday, 1973.

Farmer, K. Woman in the woods. Harrisburg, Pennsylvania: Stackpole, 1976.

*Ferber, P. (Ed.). Mountaineering: Freedom of the hills. Solana Beach, California: Craftsman's Press, 1974.

160

*Fletcher, C. The new complete walker. New York: Knopf, 1974.

Gibbs, T. Backpacking. New York: Watts, 1975.

*Hart, J. Walking softly in the wilderness. San Francisco, California: Sierra Club Books, 1977.

Herz, J. The complete backpacker. New York: Popular Library, 1973.

Highfill, K. A guide to group backpacking. Lawrence, Kansas: Author, 1974.

Jansen, C. Lightweight backpacking. Des Plaines, Illinois: Bantam, 1974.

Kelsey, R. Walking in the wild. New York: Funk & Wagnalls, 1974.

Langer, R. The joy of camping. Baltimore: Penguin Books, 1974.

Learn, R. The backpacker's digest. Chicago: Follett, n.d.

Look, D. The joy of backpacking. Sacramento, California: Jalmar Press, Press, 1975.

Lyttle, R. The complete beginner's guide to backpacking. Garden City, New York: Doubleday, 1975.

*Manning, H. Backpacking: One step at a time. New York: Vantage, 1972.

Mendenhall, R. Backpacking techniques (Rev. ed.). Glendale, California: La Siesta Press, 1973.

Merrill, B. The hikers and backpackers' handbook. New York: Winchester, 1971.

Moheny, R. The master backpacker. Harrisburg, Pennsylvania, Stackpole, 1976.

Nordic World. Snow camping. Mountainview, California, World Publications, 1974.

*Petzolt, P. The wilderness handbook. New York: Norton, 1974.

*Rethmel, R. C. Backpacking (5th ed.). Long Island City, New York: Burgess, 1974.

Riviere, B. Backcountry camping. Garden City, New York: Doubleday, 1971.

*Roberts, H. Movin' out: Equipment and techniques for eastern hikers. Lexington, Massachusetts: Stonewall Press, 1975.

Rossit, E. Snowcamping and mountaineering. New York: Funk & Wagnalls, 1970.

Rutstrum, C. Paradise below zero. Riverside, New Jersey: Macmillan, 1972.

Sajio, A. The backpacker. Totowa, New Jersey: Scribner's, 1972.

Sign Post Publications. Pack rat papers # 1. Lynwood, Washington: Author, 1972.

Sugar, A. Backpacking it. New York: Lancer, 1973.

Sullivan, G. Backpackers' handbook. New York: Grossett & Dunlop, 1972.

Walsh, M. The family wilderness handbook. Westminster, Maryland: Ballantine, 1973.

Winnett, T. Backpacking for fun. Berkeley, California: Wilderness Press, 1972.

Wood, R. Pleasure packing. Totowa, New Jersey: Condor Press, 1972.

*Van Lear, D. (Ed.). The best about backpacking. Totowa, New Jersey: Sierra Books, 1974.

POPULAR MAIL ORDER EQUIPMENT SUPPLIERS

Alpine Designs
61 85 East Arapahoe
Boulder, CO 80303

L. L. Bean
Freeport, ME 04032

Camptrails
4111 W. Clarendon
P. O. Box 23155
Phoenix, AZ 85000

Co-op Wilderness Supply
1432 University Ave.
Berkeley, CA 94702

Eastern Mountain Sports
1041 Commonwealth Ave.
Boston, MA 02215

Frostline, Inc.
Dept. C
Frostline Circle
Denver, CO 80241

Great World, Inc.
250 Farm Village Rd.
West Simsbury, CT 06092

Houlubar
Box 7
Boulder, CO 80302

Kelty
1801 Victory Blvd.
Glendale, CA 91201

Moor & Mountain
63 Park St.
Andover, MA 01810

Mountain Safety Research, Inc.
631 S. 96th St.
Seattle, WA 98108

The North Face
1234   5th St.
Berkeley, CA 94710

Paul Petzolt Wilderness Equipment
P. O. Box 78
Lander, WY 82520

Recreational Equipment, Inc.
1525   11th Ave.
Seattle, WA 98122

Sierra Designs, Inc.
247 Fourth St.
Oakland, CA 94607

Ski Hut
1615 University Ave.
Berkeley, CA 94703

Stephenson's
RFD 4
Box 398
Gilford, NH 03246

ABOUT THE AUTHOR

   Chuck Gormley is currently the Coordinator of Outdoor Recreation for the University of California at San Diego. He has a Masters Degree in Outdoor Education as well as Bachelor Degrees in Forestry and Environmental Studies.

   For the past ten years Chuck has been actively involved in various volunteer and professional organizations concerned with outdoor recreation and environmental protection.

   Aside from backpacking, Chuck leads activities in canoeing, cross-country skiing, rock climbing and winter mountaineering.